Christmas Music for Easy Guitar Volume One

Robert Anthony

Instructional video links will be posted at:

www.RobertAnthonyPublishing.com

as videos are produced.

If this book is helping you, please post a positive review at whichever website you had purchased it from. If you have questions, suggestions, or constructive criticism, feel free to use the email link on my site to let me know.

©2022 Robert Anthony Publishing. All Rights Reserved.

Also Available

Angels From the Realms of Glory, Auld Lang Syne, Carol of the Bells, Hallelujah Chorus, The Holly and the Ivy, The Twelve Days of Christmas, and 17 more!

Also Available at:
www.RobertAnthonyPublishing.com

Foreword:

Christmas Music for Easy Guitar is now available as Volume One and Volume Two.

Each song in both volumes is arranged in four ways:
1. Single-note melody with tablature (easy).
2. Chord-melody with tablature (more advanced).
3. Single-note melody with only standard notation.
4. Chord-melody with only standard notation.

I use the standard notation arrangements to train my own guitar students to improve their ability to read music for guitar, but many guitar players will surely prefer to use the tablature arrangements to learn the songs.

If you can not yet read standard notation, or would like to improve that skill set, the book 300 Progressive Sight Reading Exercises for Guitar will help you enormously. There are links on my webpage for this book, and to a set of free video lessons to help you get started acquiring your reading skills.

www.RobertAnthonyPublishing.com

Lyrics are appropriately included for convenience, for this book is meant to train guitar and musical skill — not to be a collection of sing-along arrangements.

~ Robert Anthony

Table of Contents

- 6 Angels We Have Heard on High
- 12 Away in a Manger
- 18 Deck the Halls
- 24 Ding Dong! Merrily on High
- 32 The First Noel
- 38 Go Tell it on the Mountain
- 44 God Rest Ye Merry Gentlemen
- 50 Hark! The Herald Angels Sing
- 56 It Came Upon the Midnight Clear
- 62 Jingle Bells
- 70 Joy to the World
- 76 O Christmas Tree
- 82 O Come All Ye Faithful
- 88 O Come, O Come, Emmanuel
- 94 O Holy Night
- 100 O Little Town of Bethlehem
- 106 Silent Night
- 112 Up On the Housetop
- 118 We Three Kings
- 124 We Wish You a Merry Christmas
- 130 What Child is This?
- 136 While Shepherds Watched Their Flocks

Angels We Have Heard on High

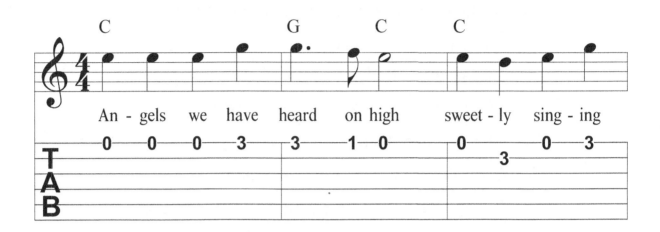
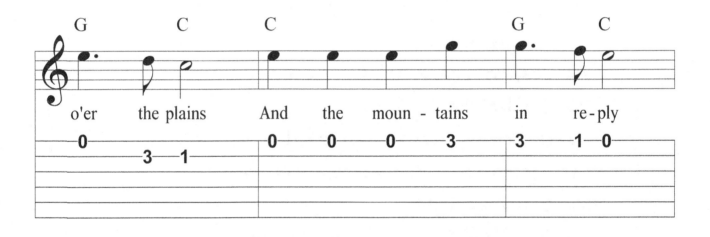
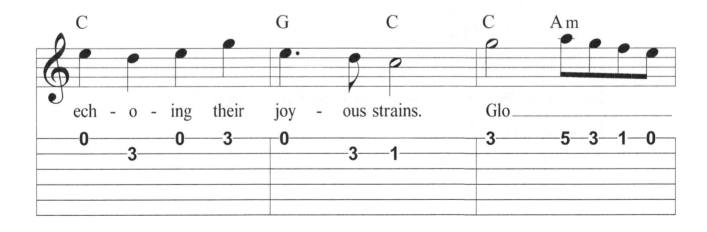

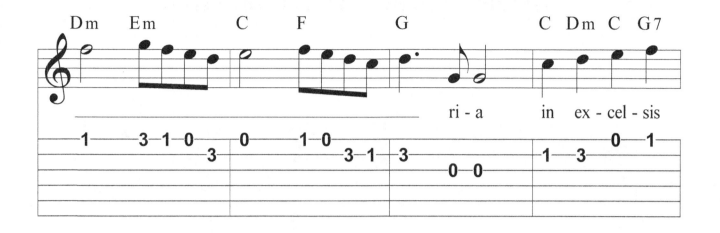
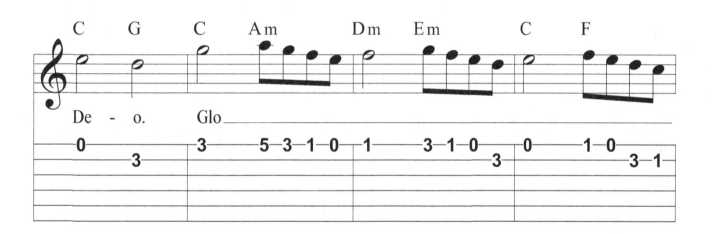
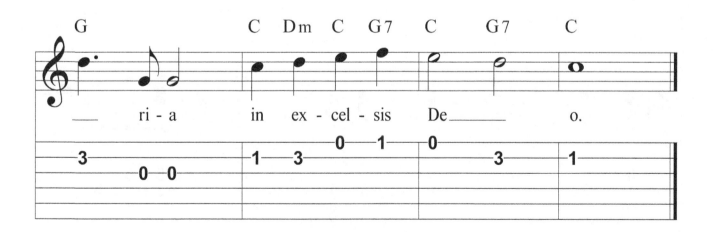

Angels We Have Heard on High

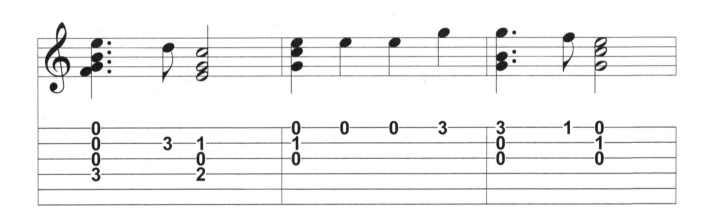
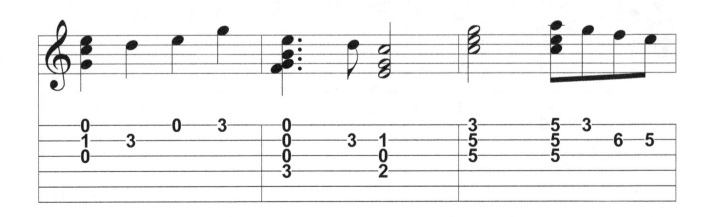

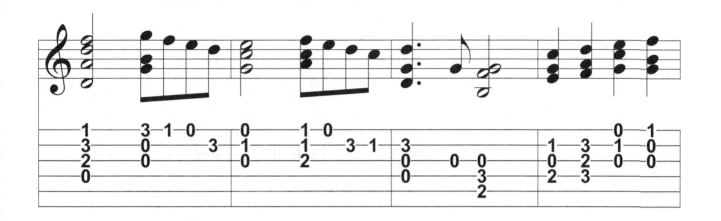
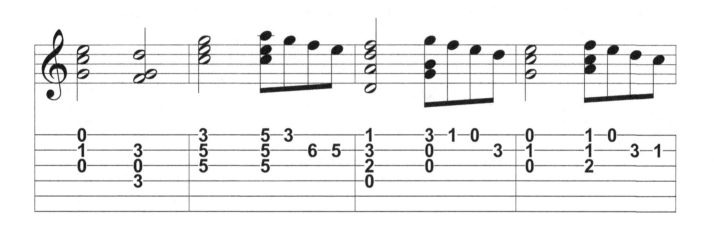
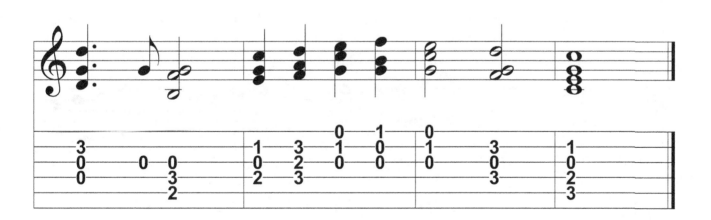

Angels We Have Heard on High

Angels We Have Heard on High

Away in a Manger

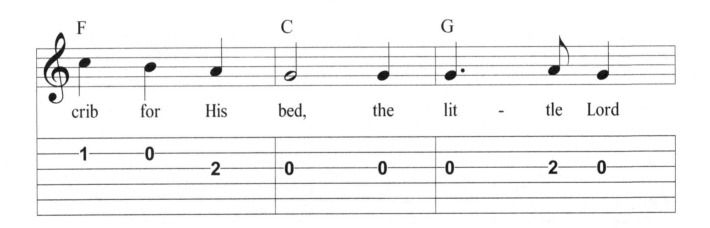
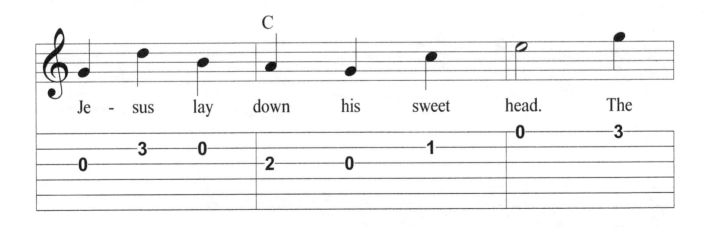

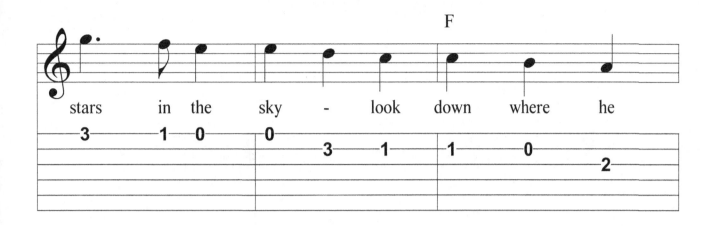
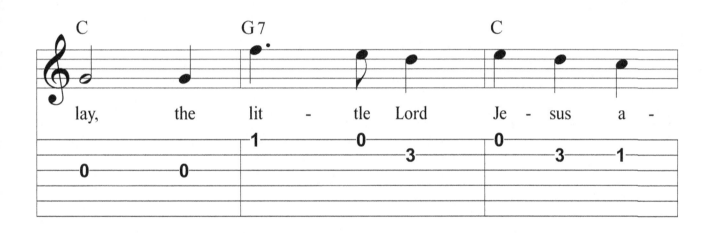
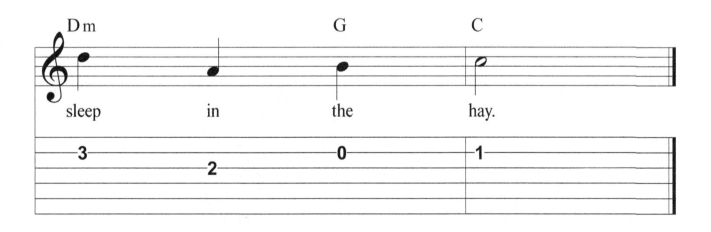

Away in a Manger

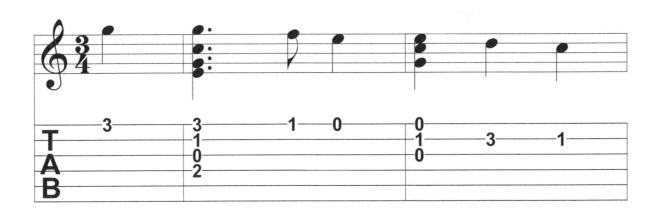
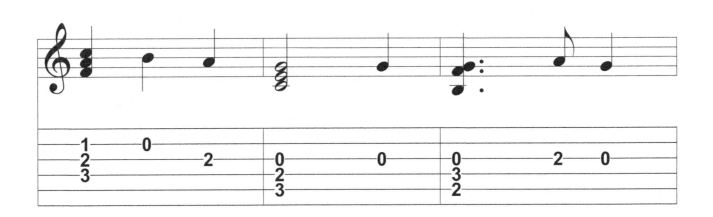

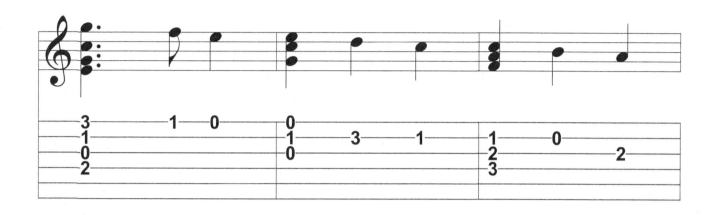
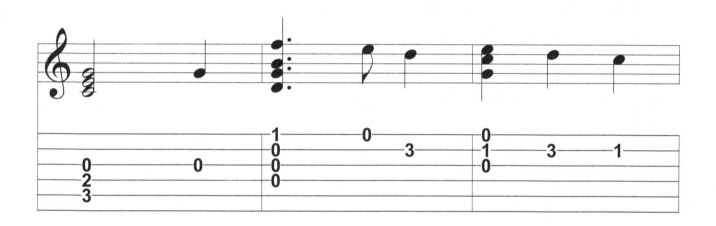
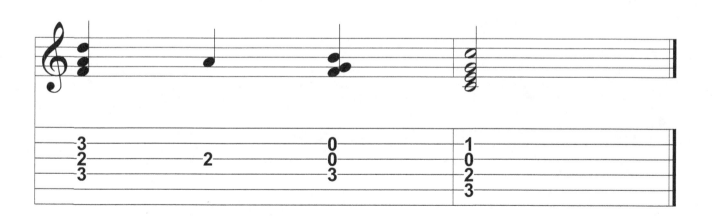

Away in a Manger

Away in a Manger

Deck the Halls

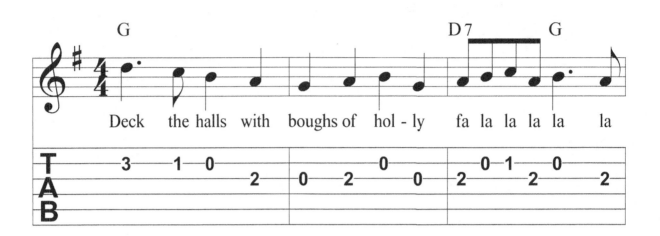
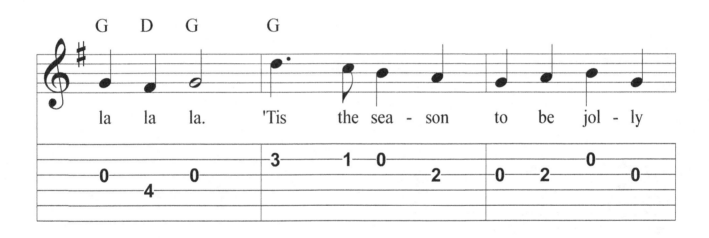
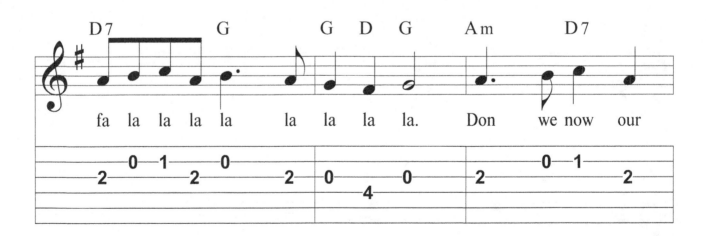

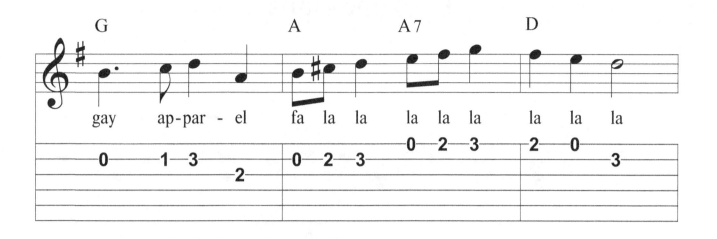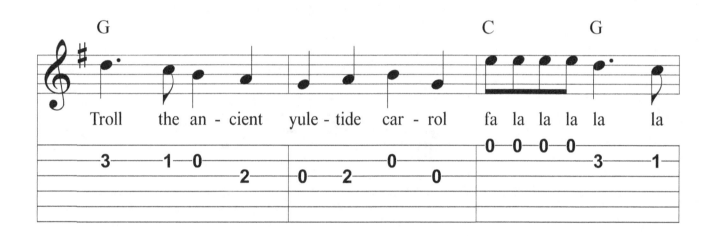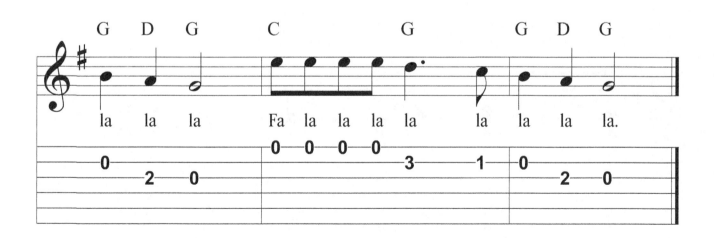

Deck the Halls

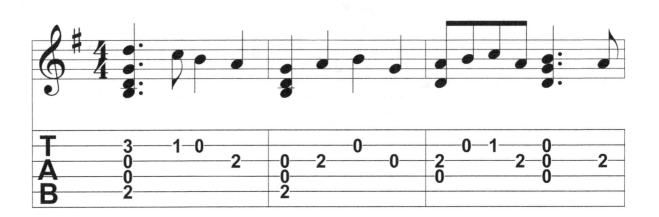
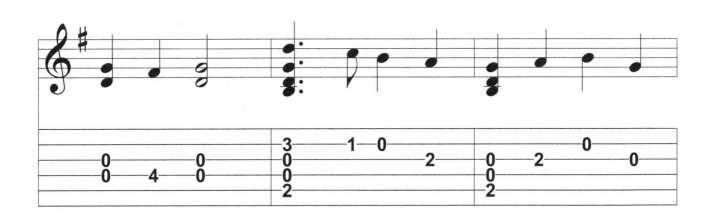

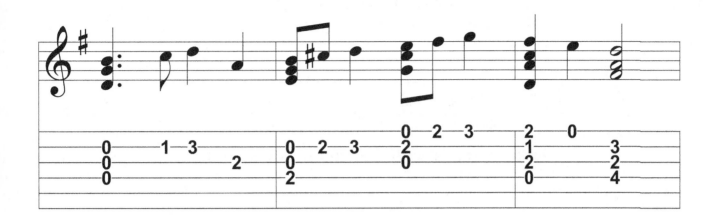
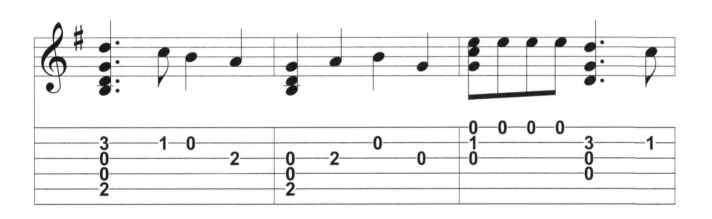
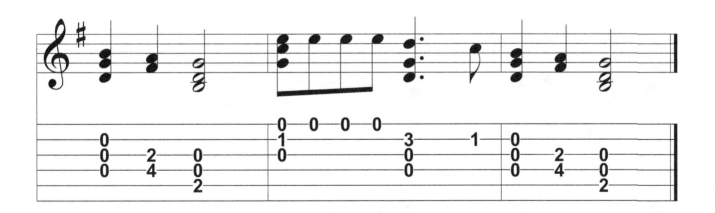

Deck the Halls

Deck the Halls

Ding Dong! Merrily on High

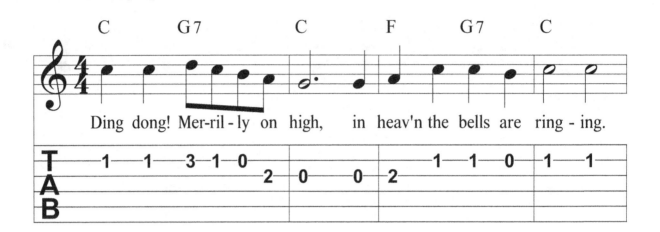

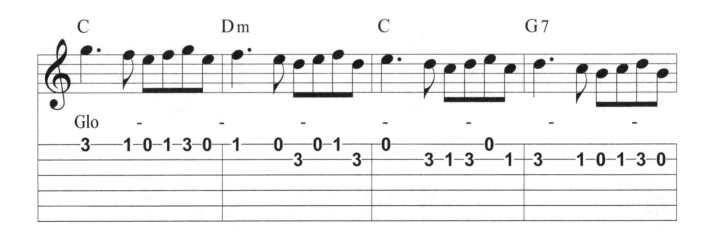

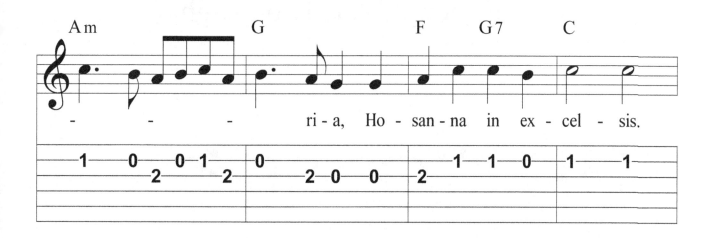
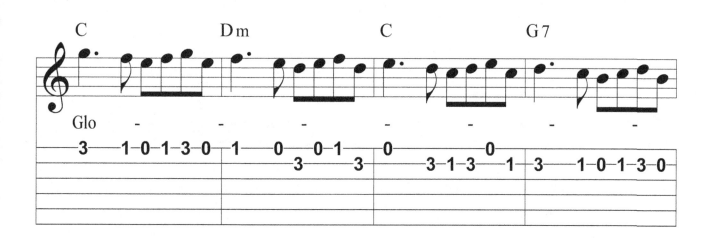
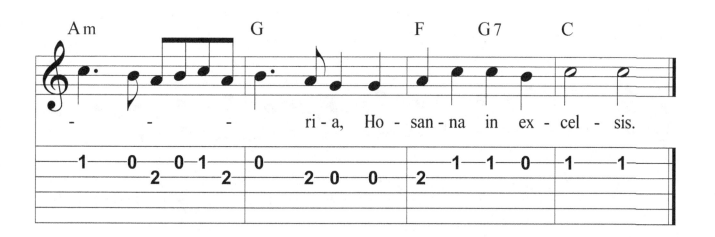

Ding Dong! Merrily on High

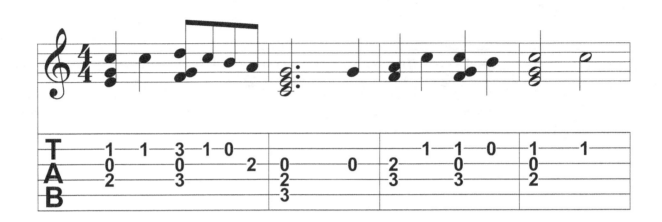
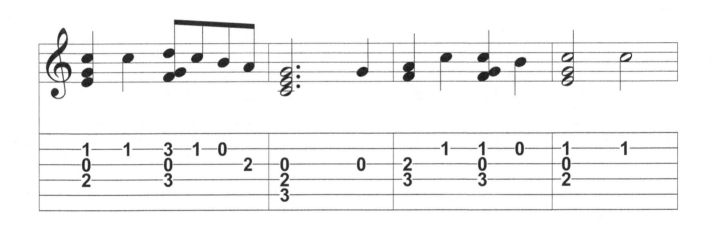
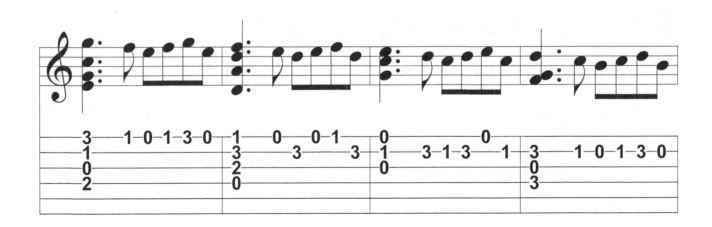

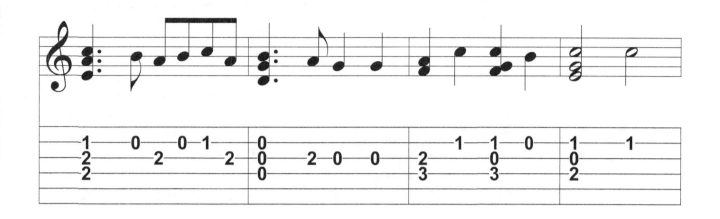
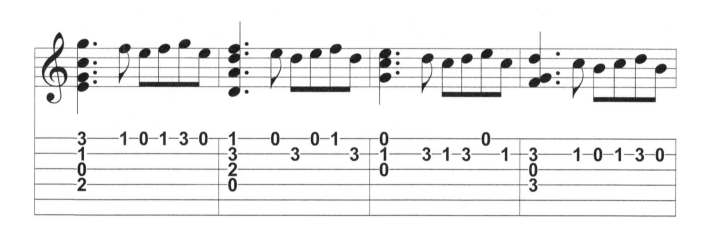
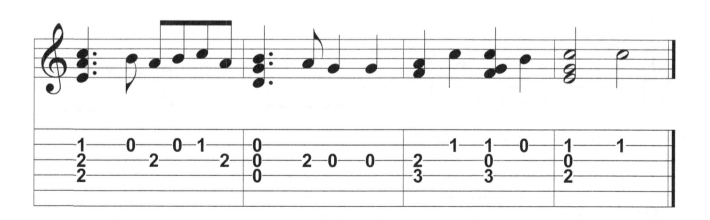

Ding Dong! Merrily on High

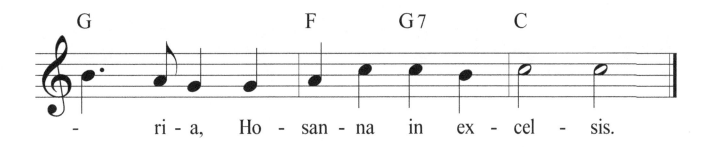

Ding Dong! Merrily on High

The First Noel

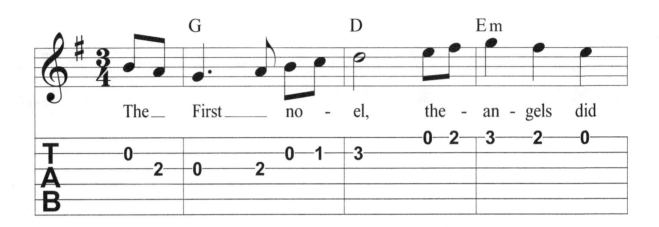
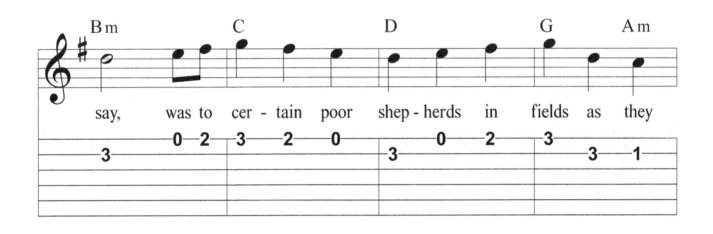
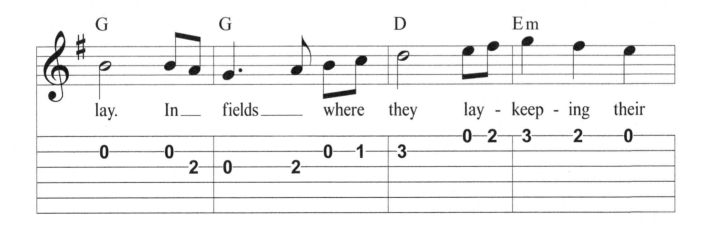

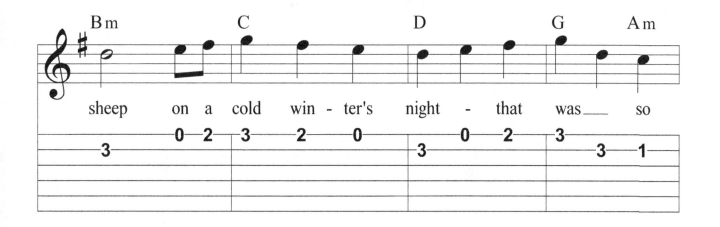
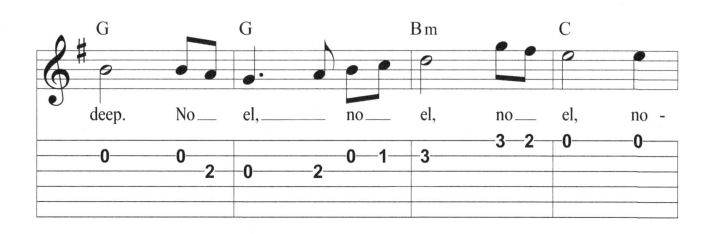
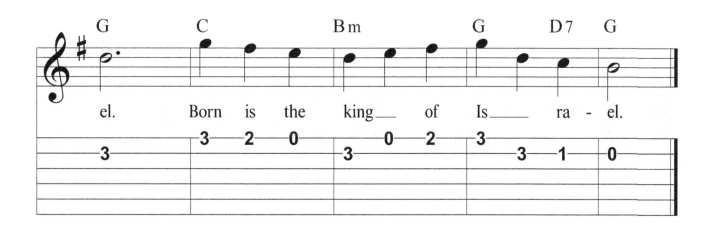

The First Noel

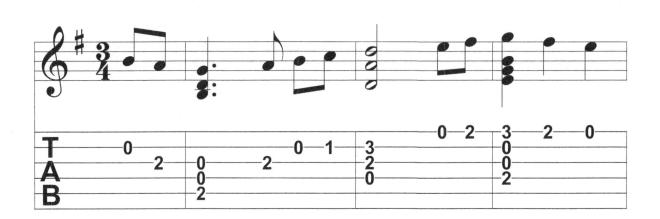
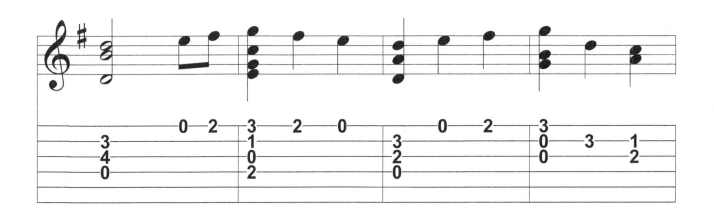
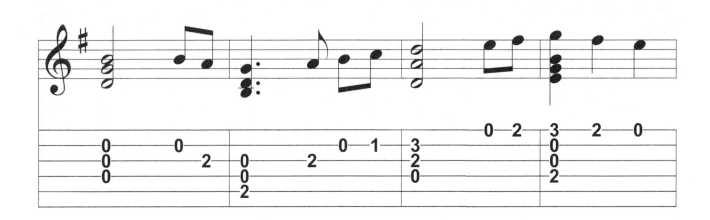

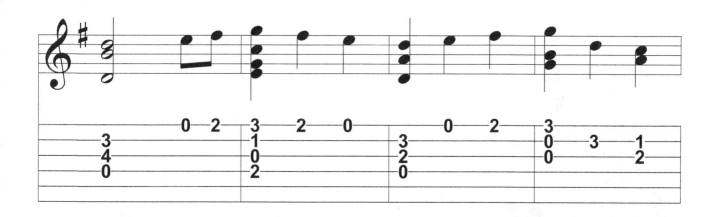
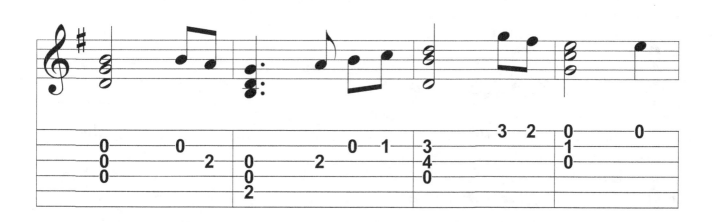

The First Noel

The First Noel

Go Tell it on the Mountain

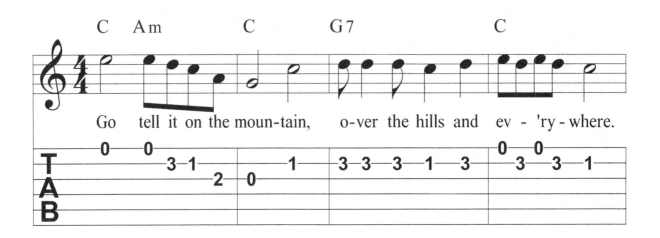
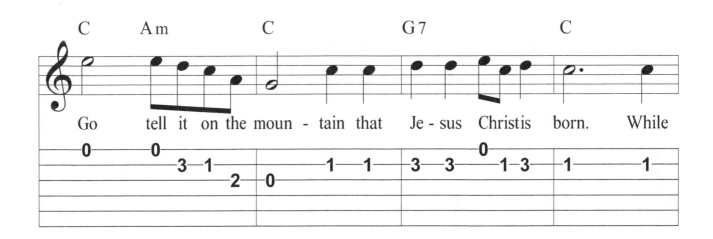
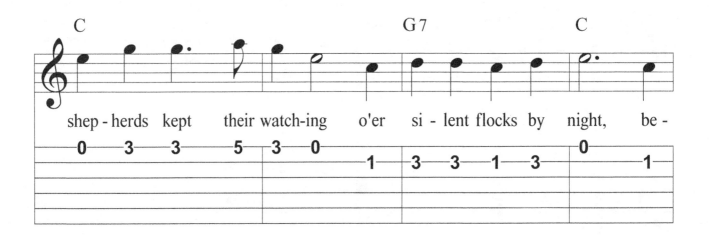

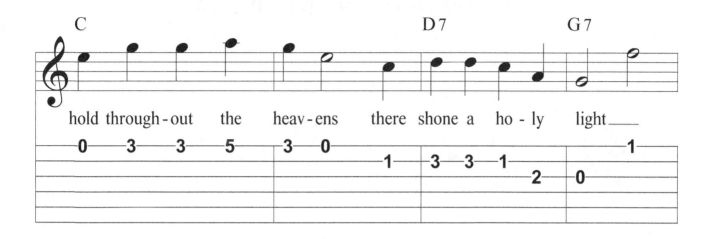
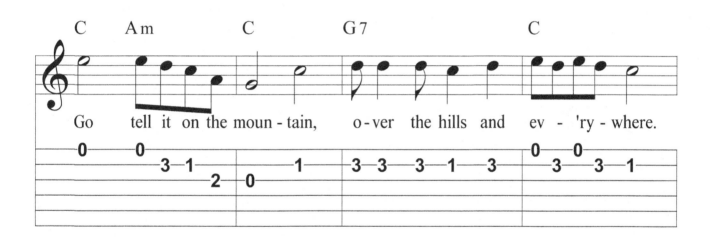
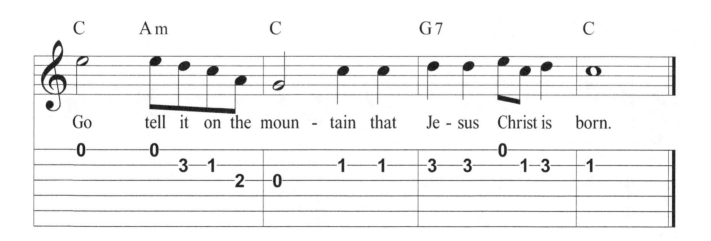

Go Tell it on the Mountain

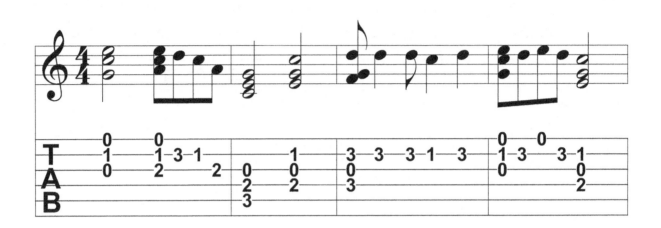

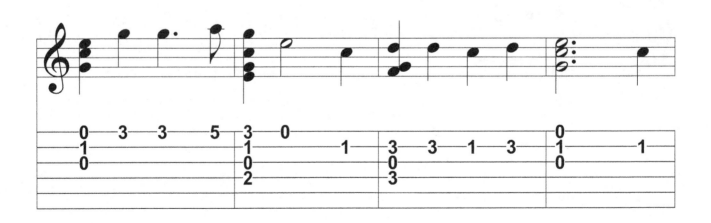

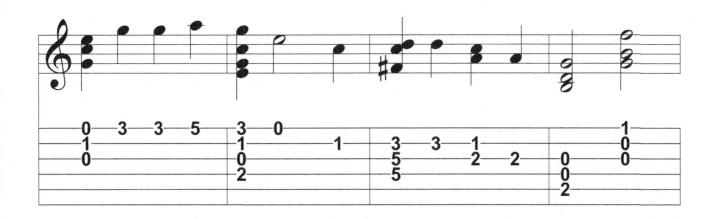
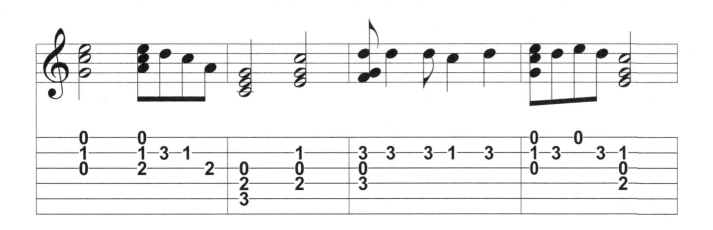
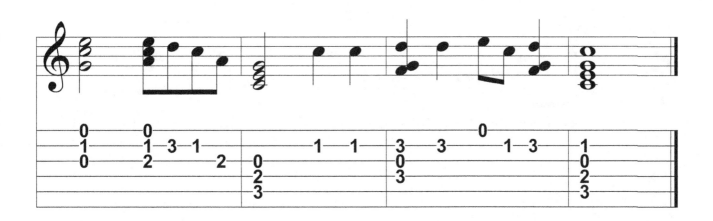

Go Tell it on the Mountain

Go Tell it on the Mountain

43

God Rest Ye Merry Gentlemen

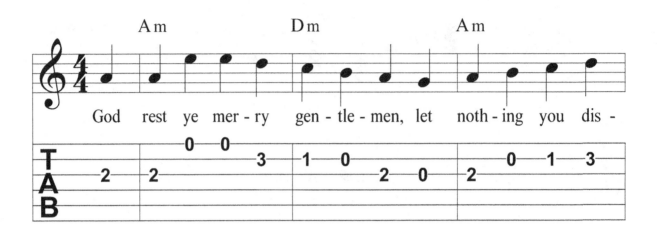
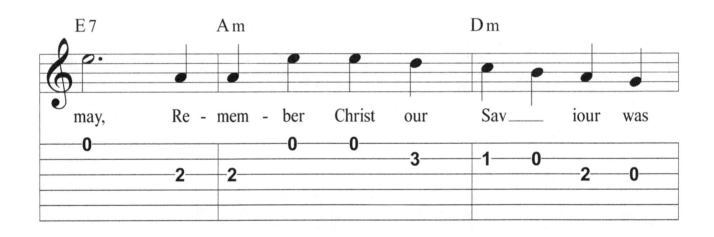
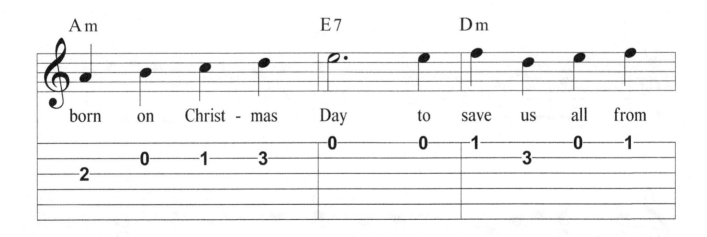

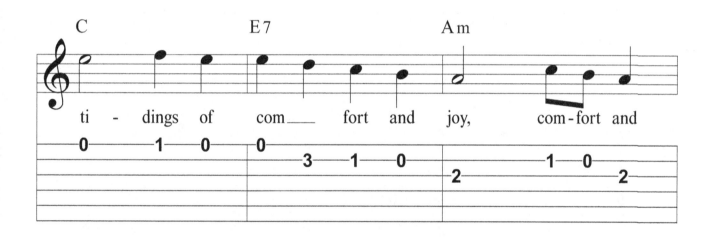
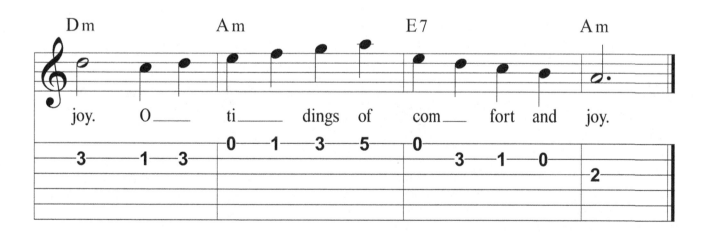

God Rest Ye Merry Gentlemen

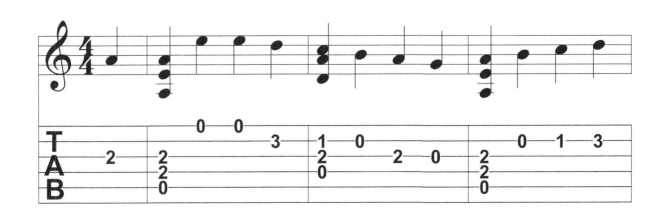
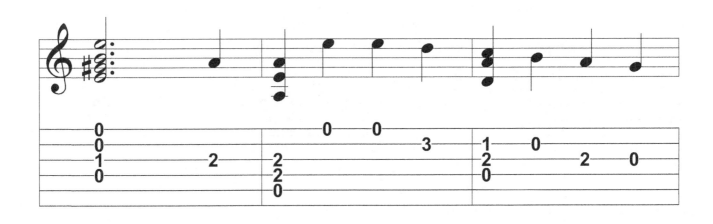
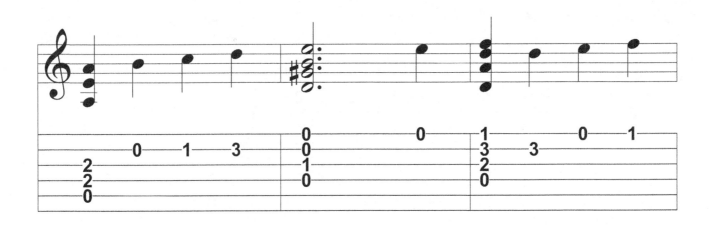

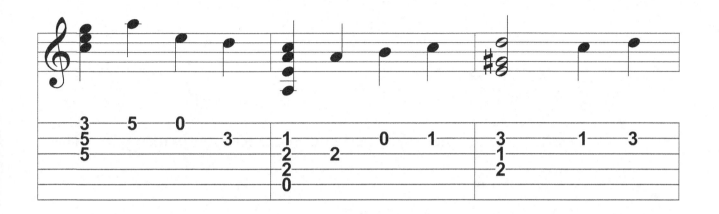
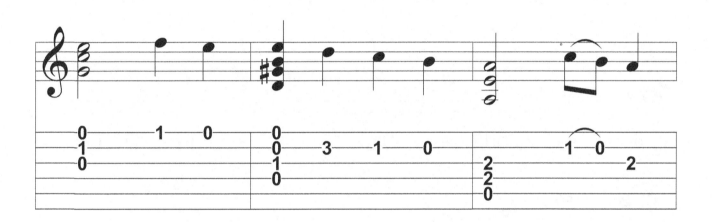
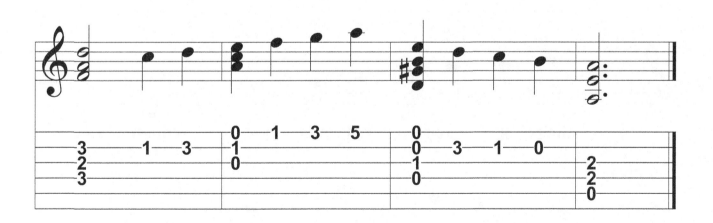

God Rest Ye Merry Gentlemen

God Rest Ye Merry Gentlemen

Hark! The Herald Angels Sing

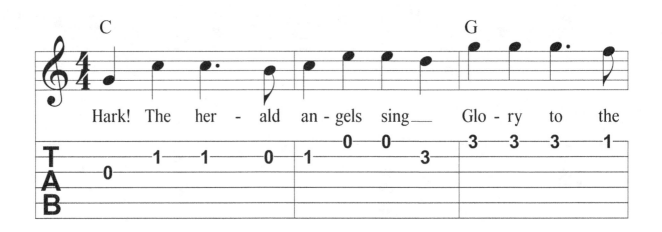
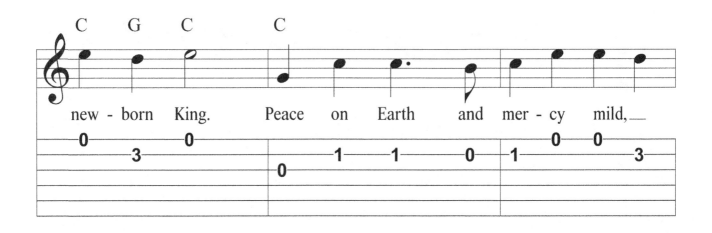
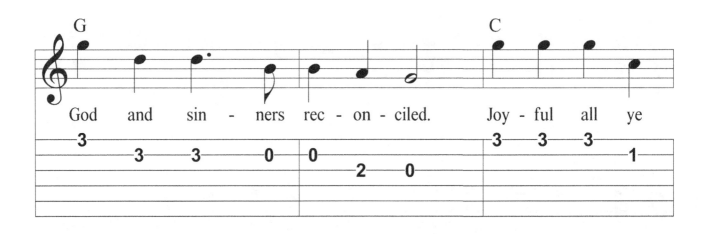

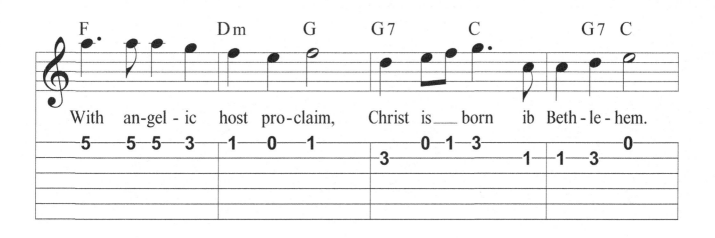
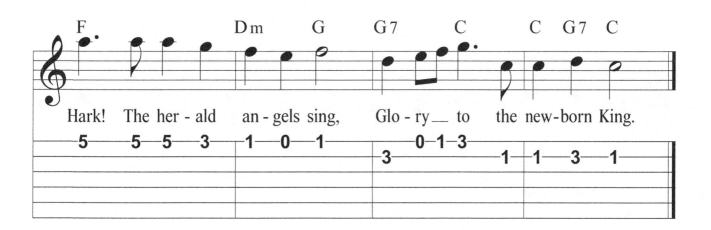

Hark! The Herald Angels Sing

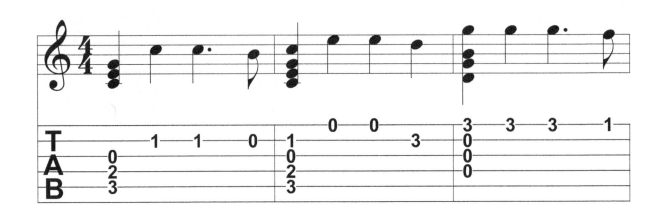
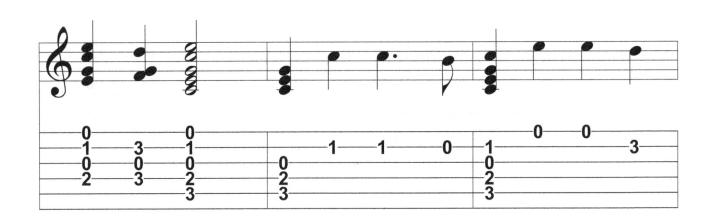
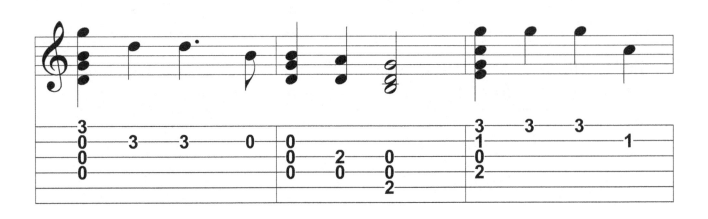

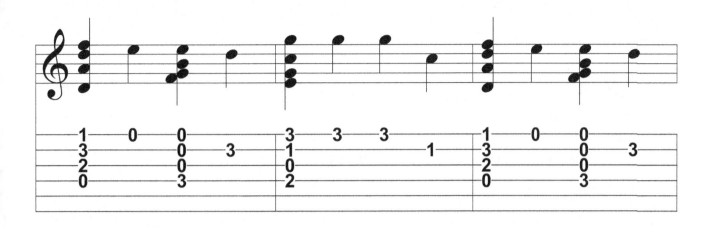
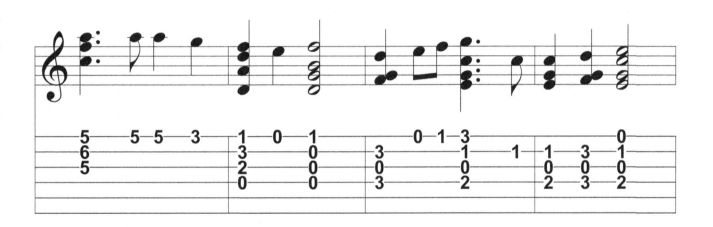
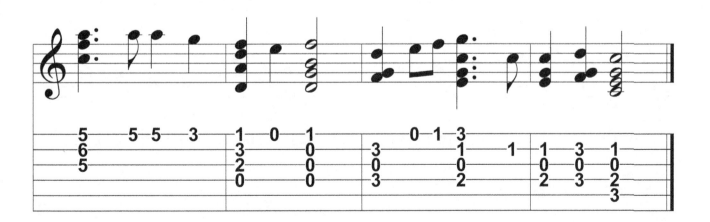

Hark! The Herald Angels Sing

Hark! The Herald Angels Sing

It Came Upon the Midnight Clear

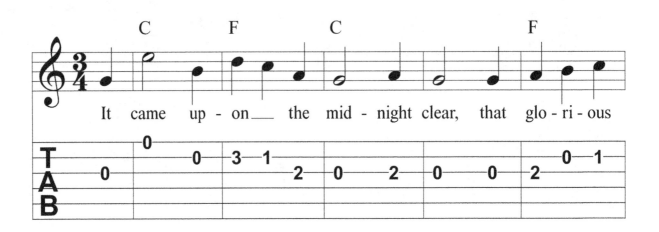
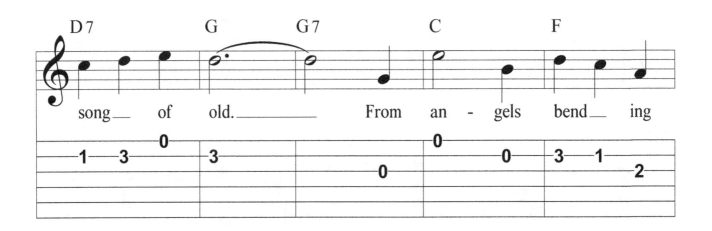
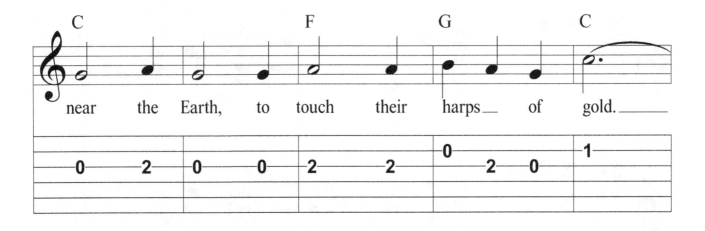

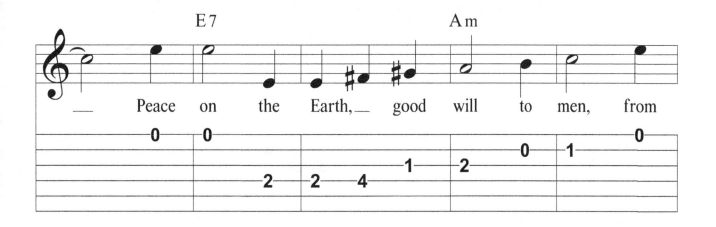
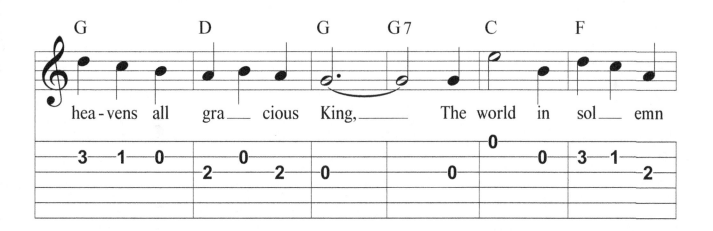
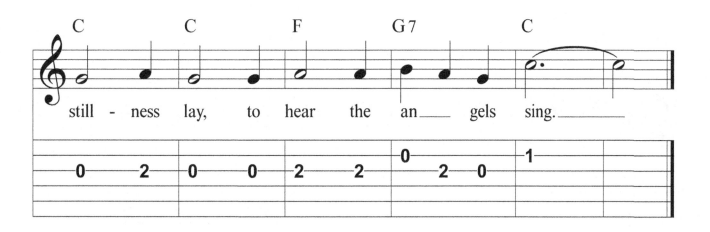

It Came Upon the Midnight Clear

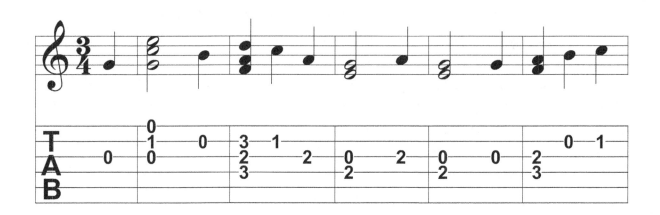
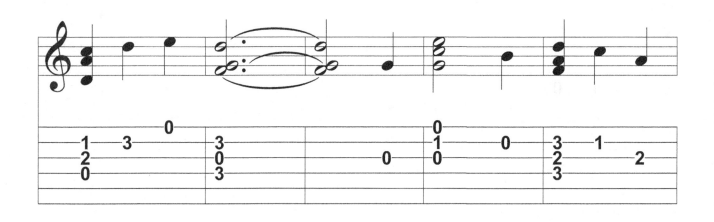
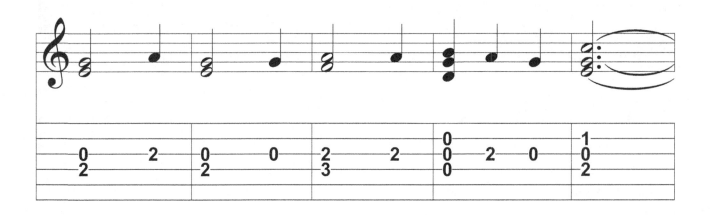

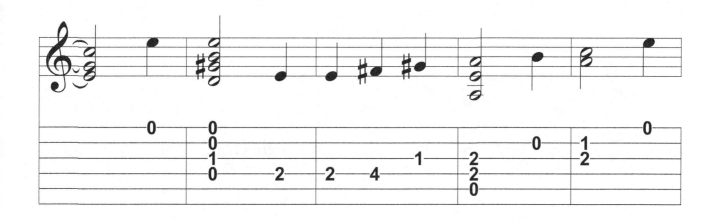
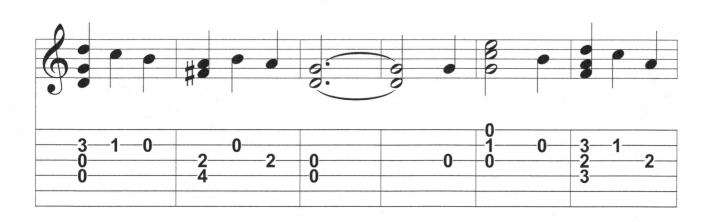
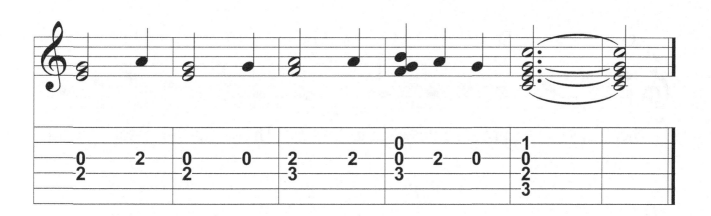

It Came Upon the Midnight Clear

It Came Upon the Midnight Clear

Jingle Bells

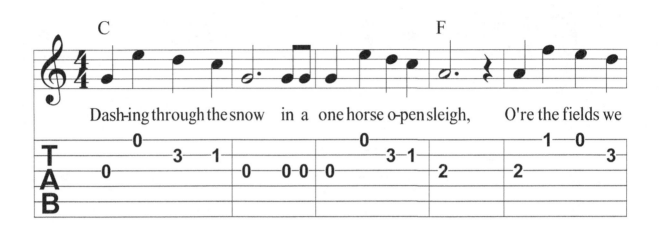
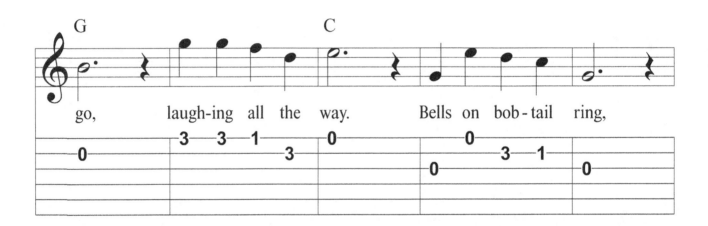
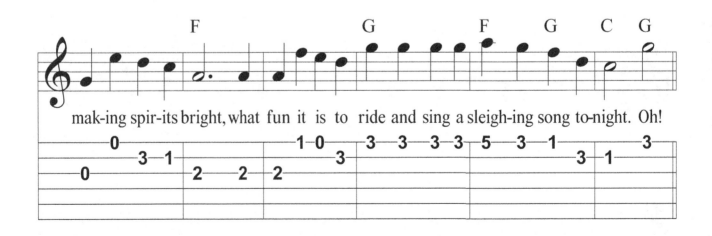

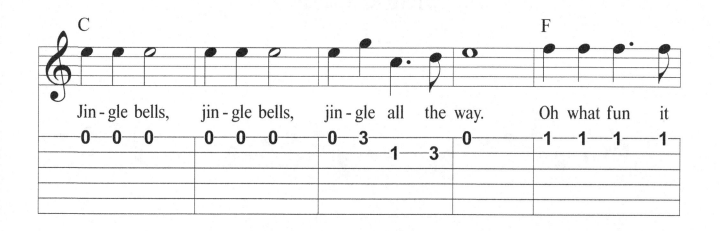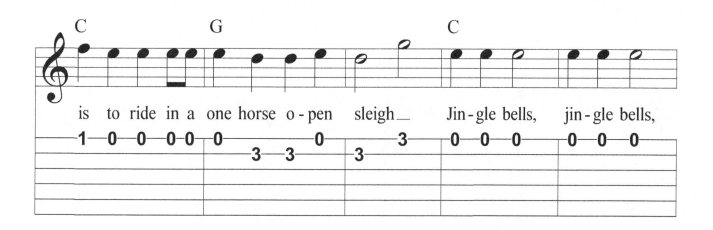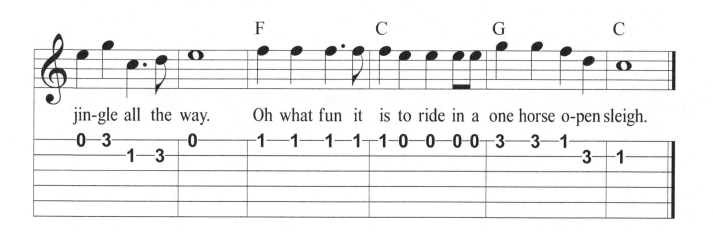

Jingle Bells

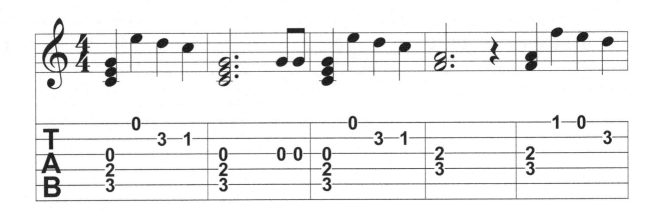
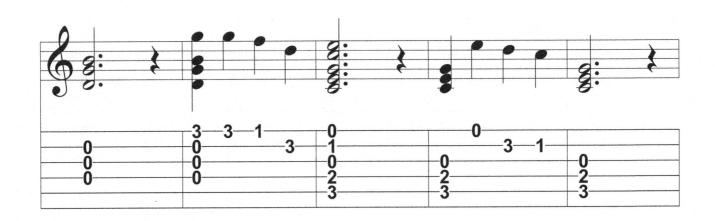

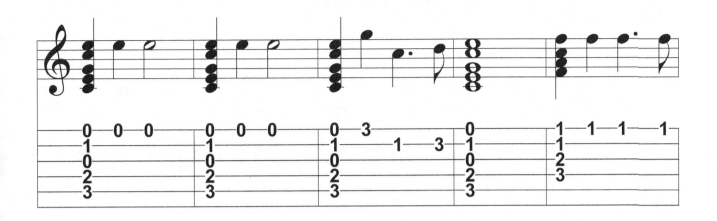
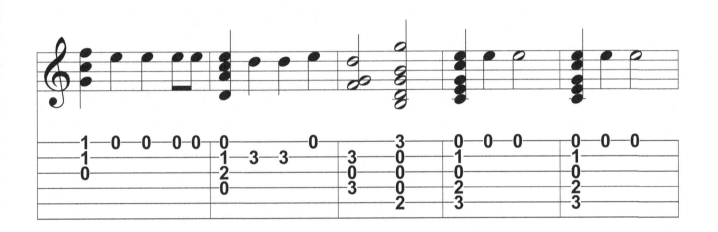

65

Jingle Bells

Jingle Bells

Also Available

Joy to the World

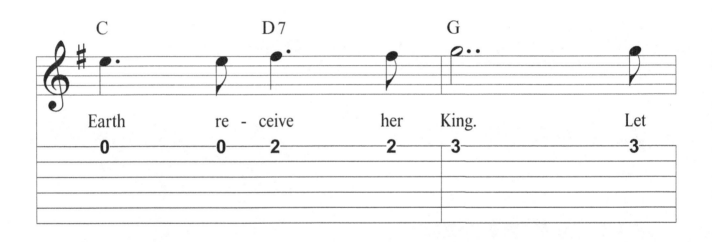

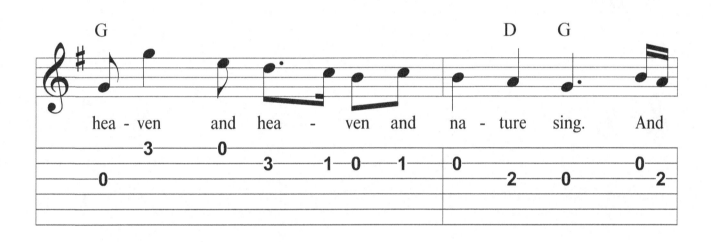

Joy to the World

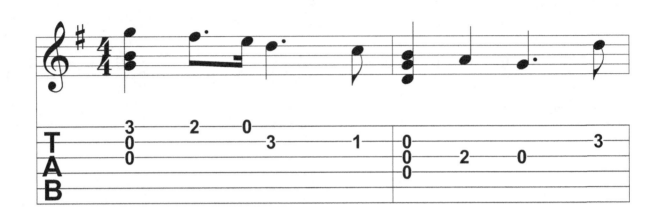

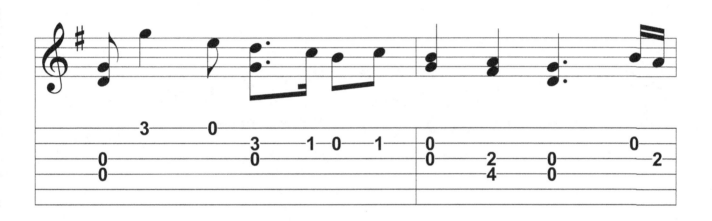
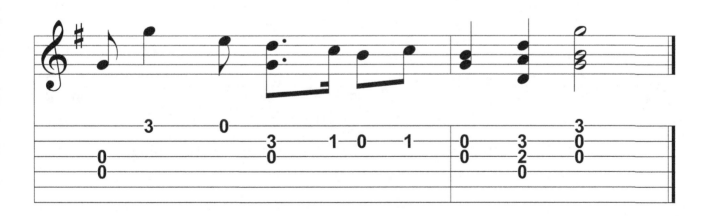

Joy to the World

74

Joy to the World

O Christmas Tree

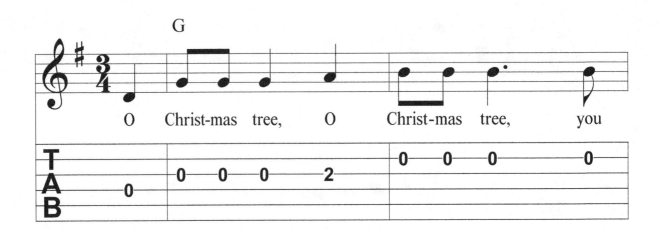
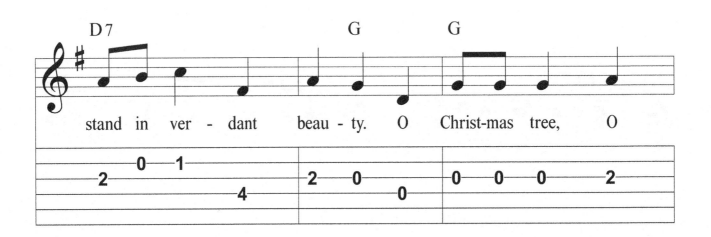

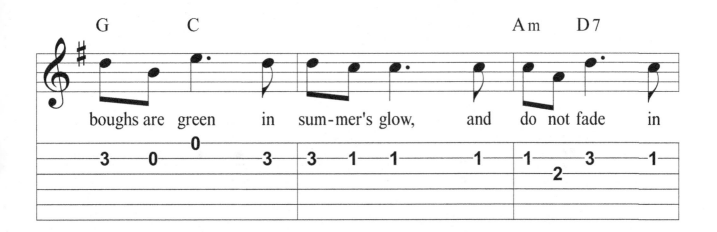
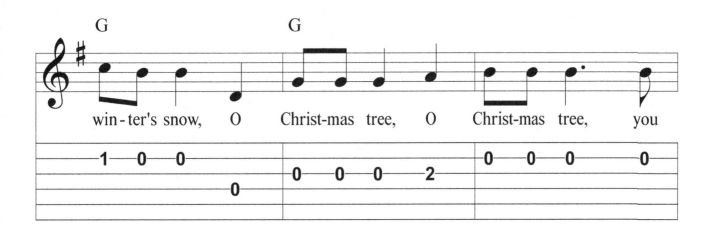
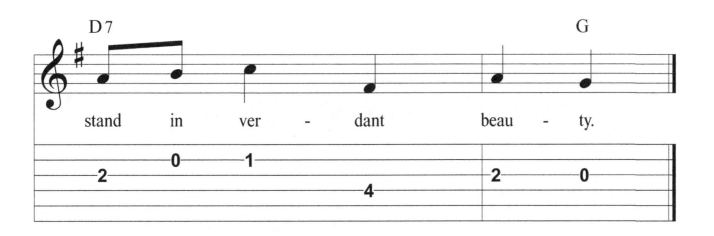

O Christmas Tree

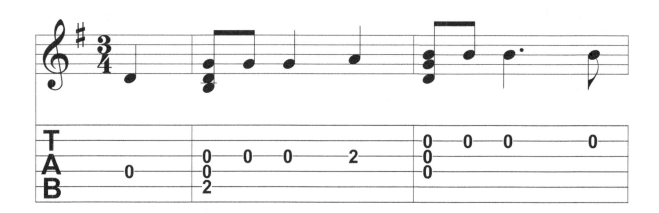

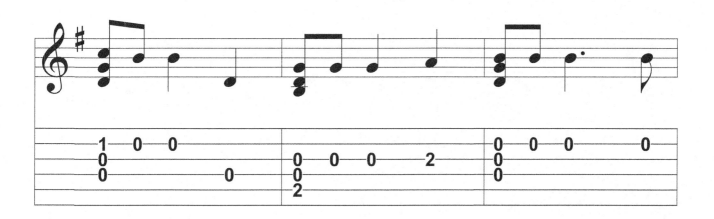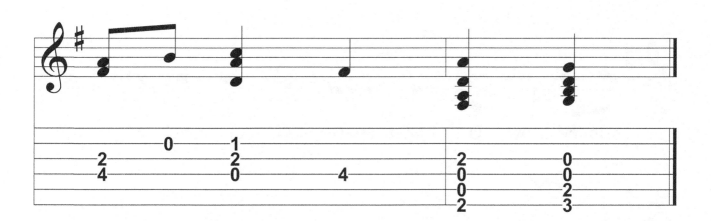

O Christmas Tree

O Christmas Tree

81

O Come All Ye Faithful

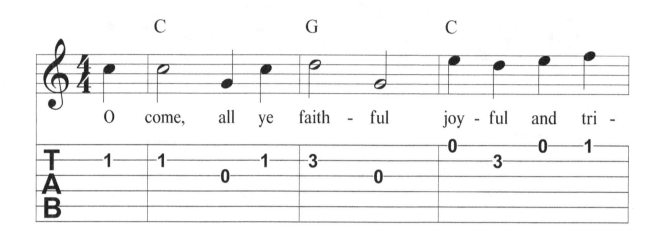
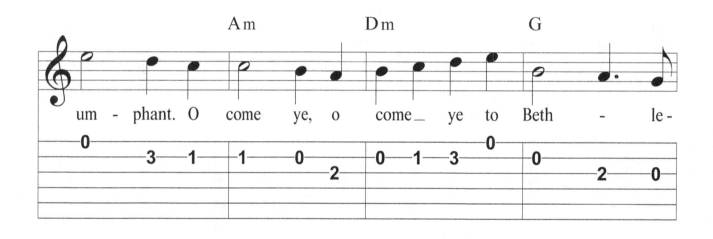
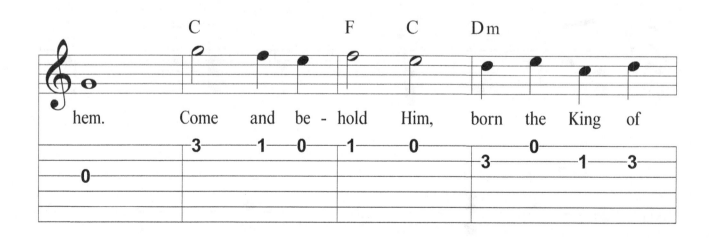

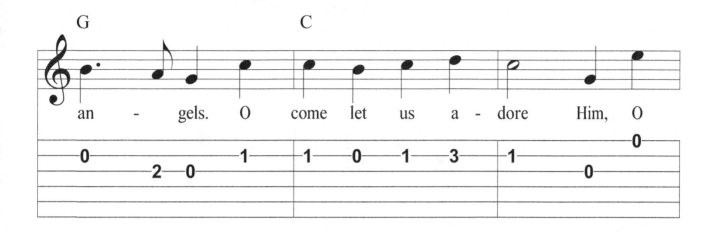
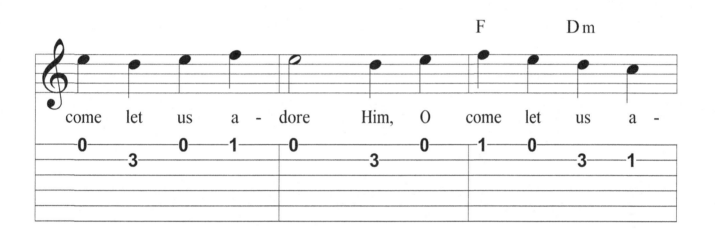
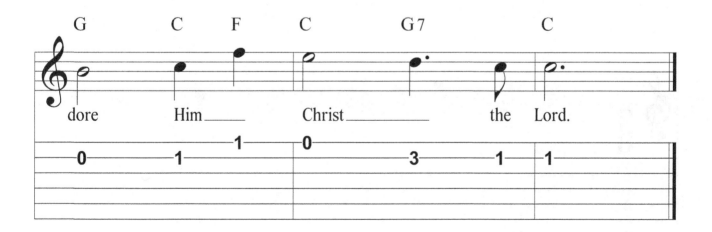

O Come All Ye Faithful

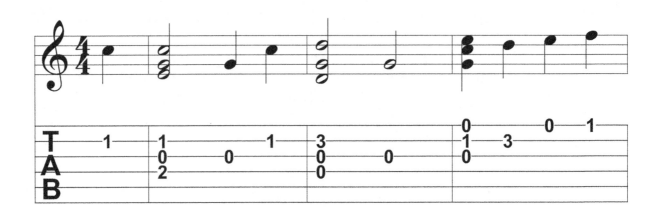
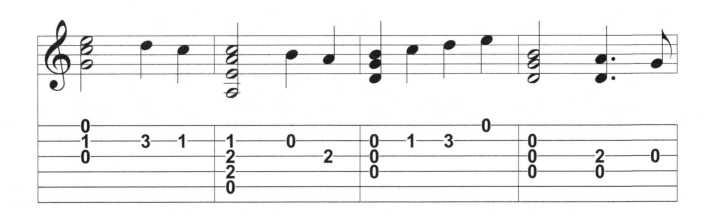
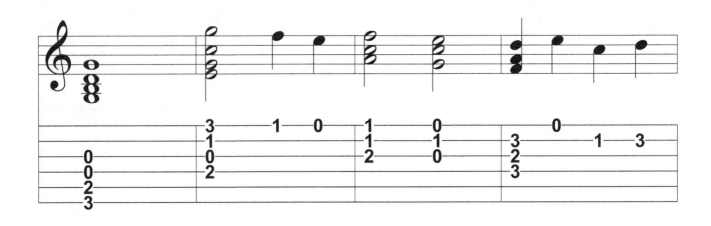

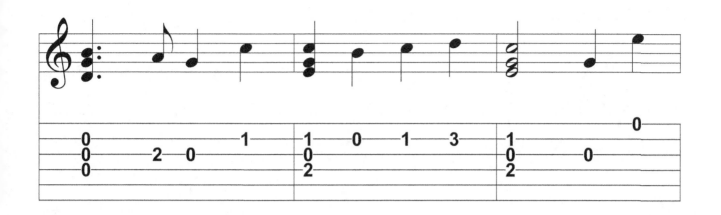
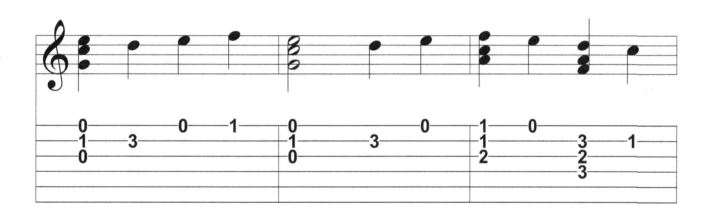
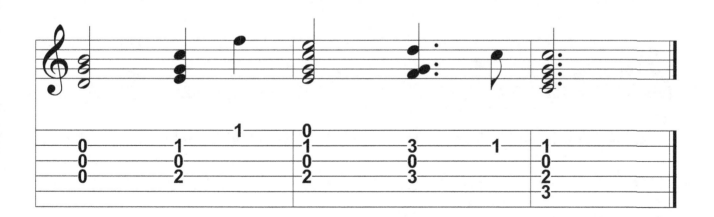

O Come All Ye Faithful

O Come All Ye Faithful

O Come, O Come, Emmanuel

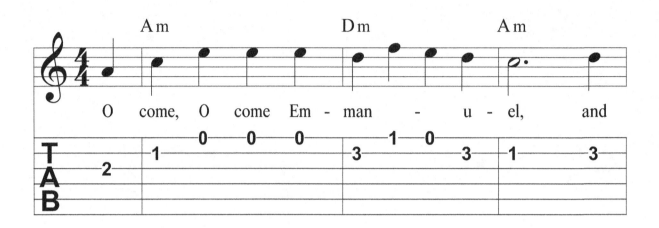
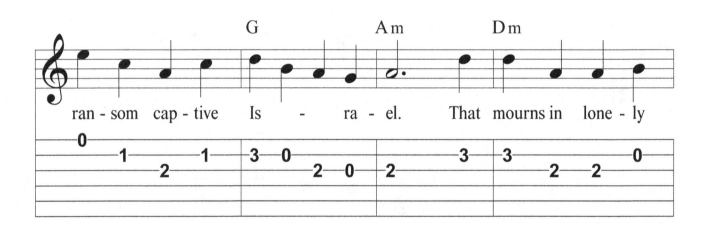
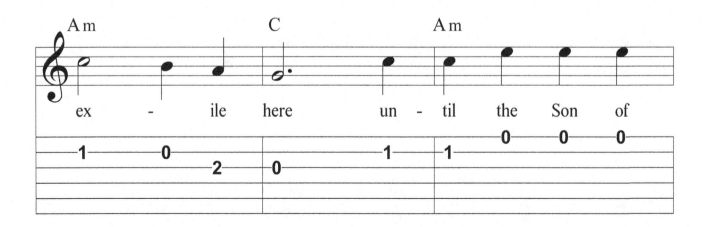

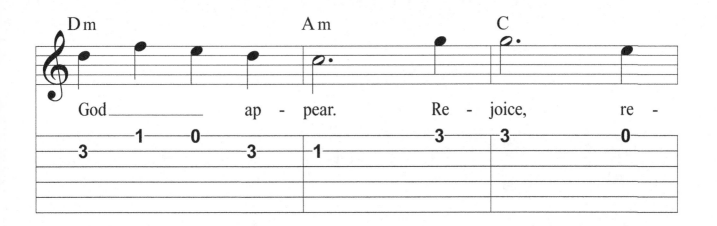
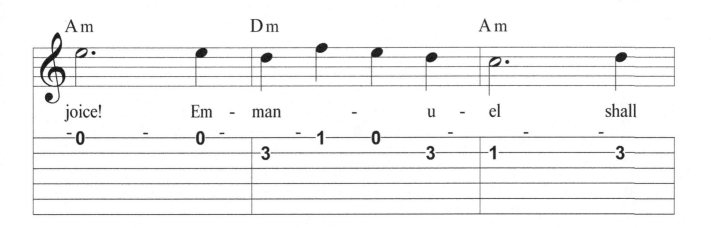
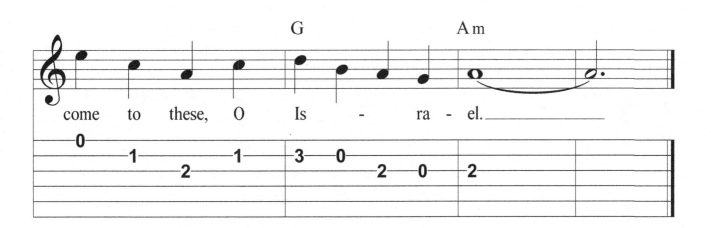

O Come, O Come, Emmanuel

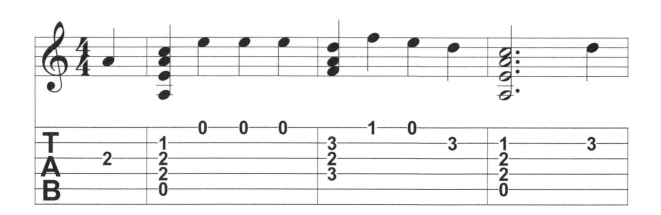
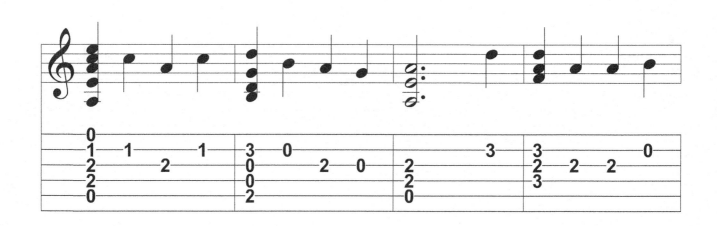
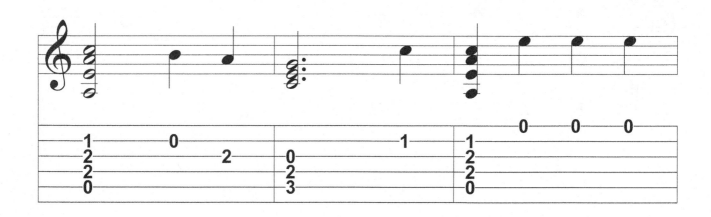

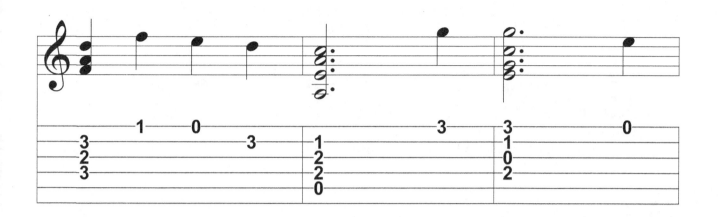
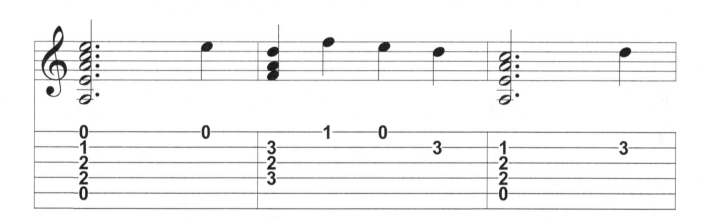
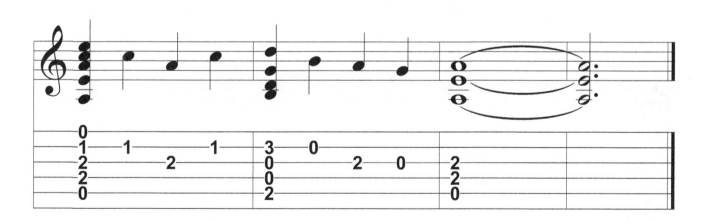

O Come, O Come, Emmanuel

O Come, O Come, Emmanuel

O Holy Night

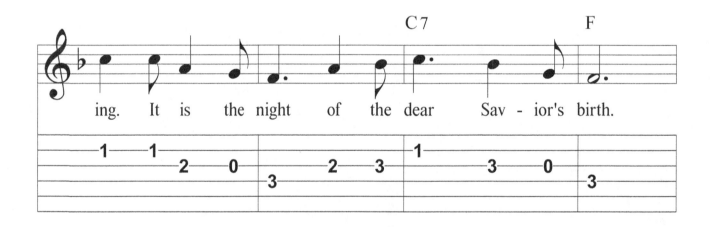
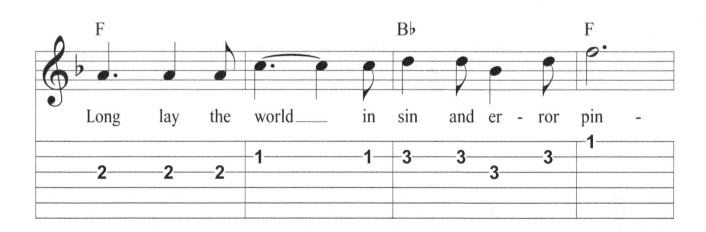

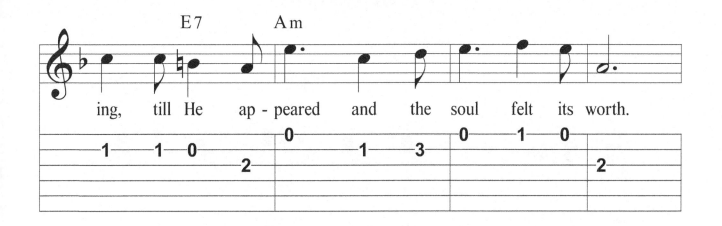

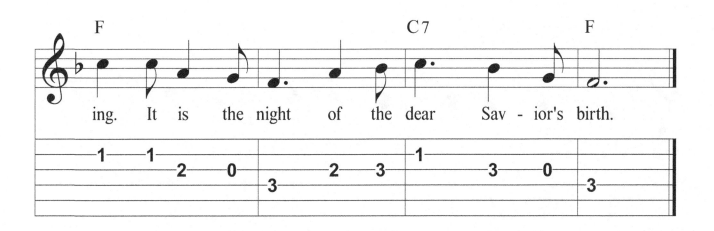

O Holy Night

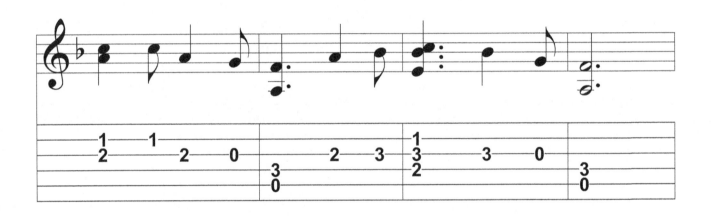

O Holy Night

O Holy Night

O Little Town of Bethlehem

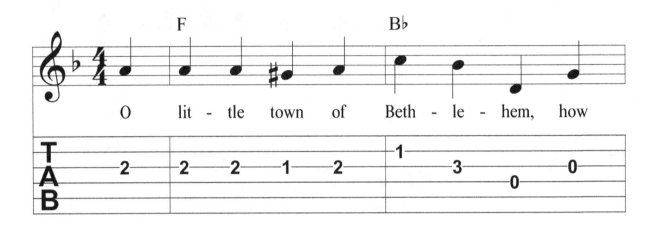
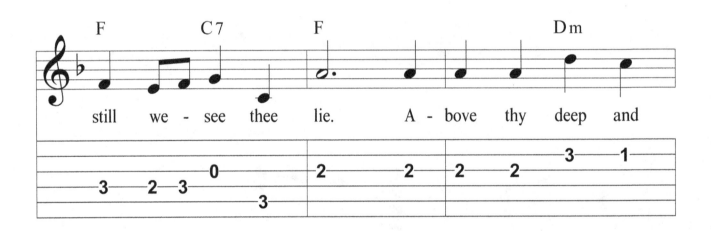
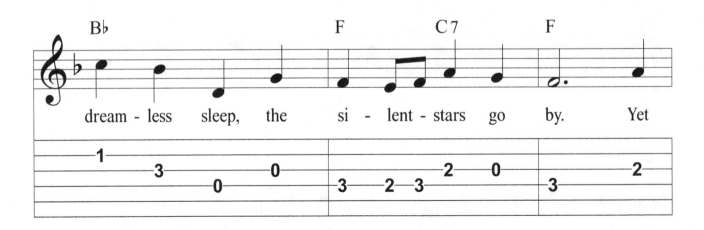

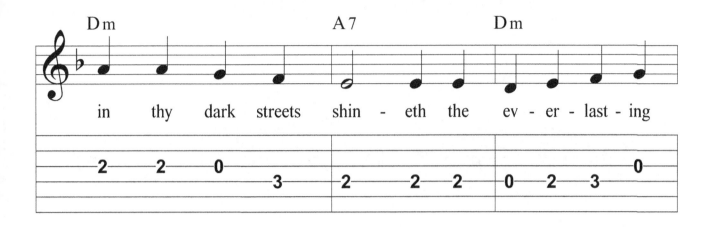
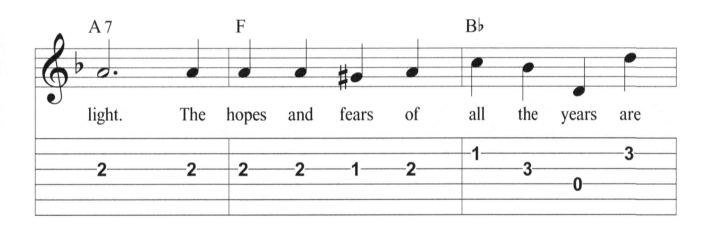
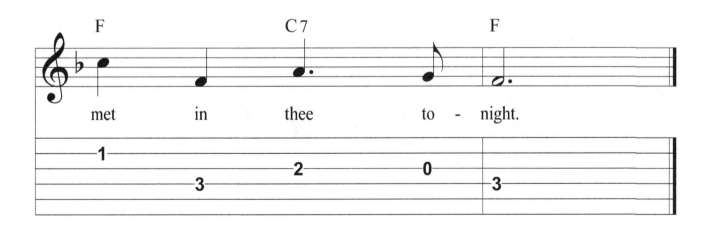

O Little Town of Bethlehem

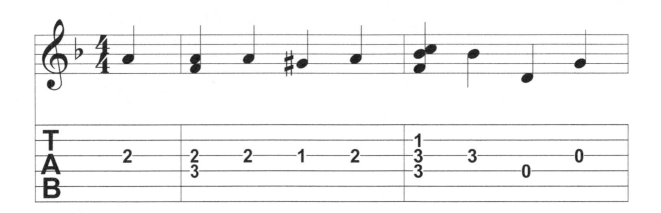
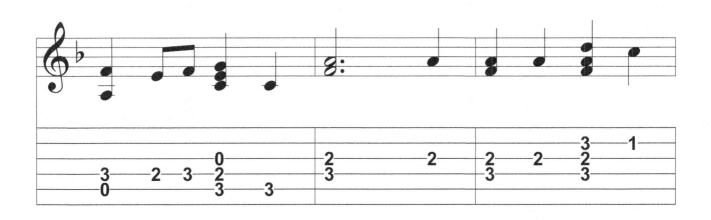
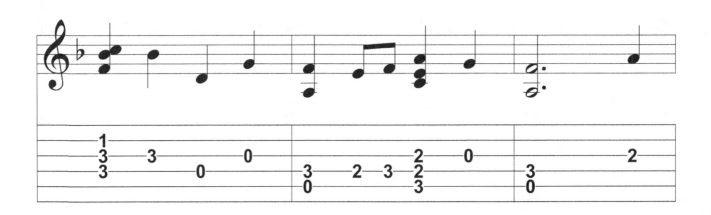

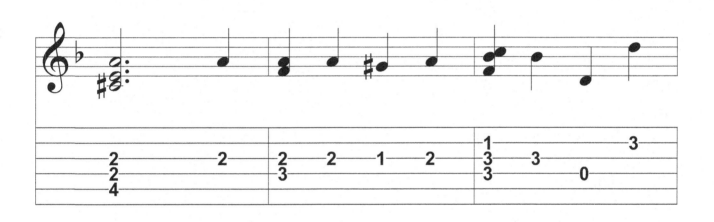
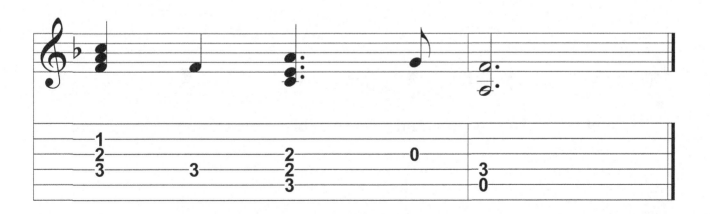

O Little Town of Bethlehem

O Little Town of Bethlehem

Silent Night

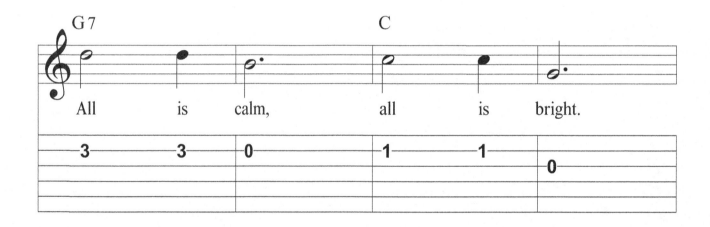
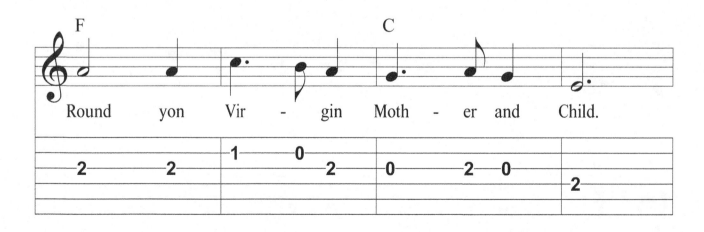

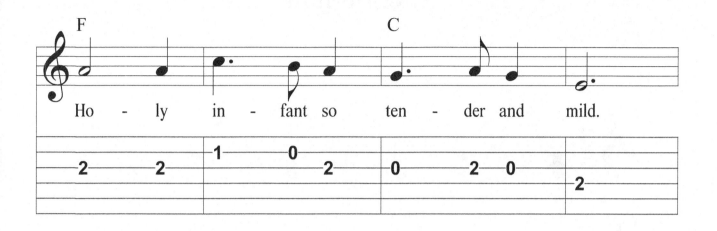
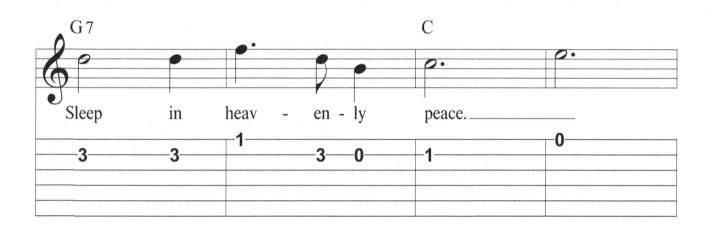
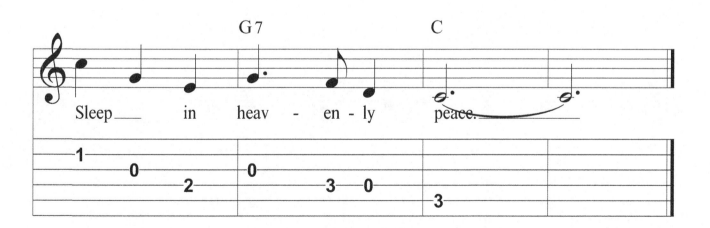

Silent Night

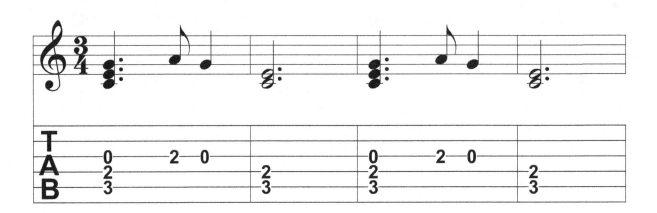
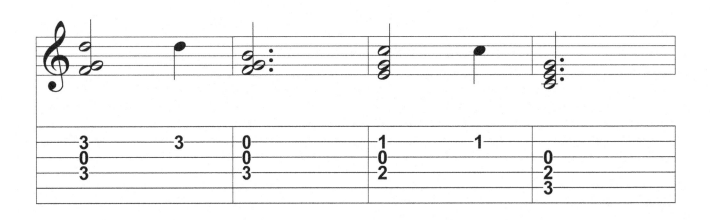
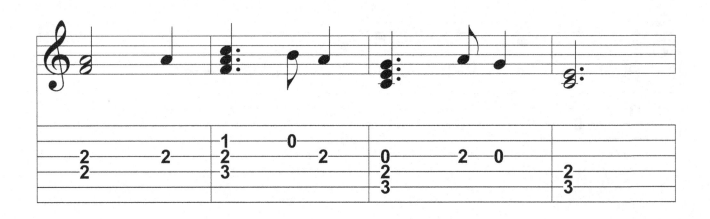

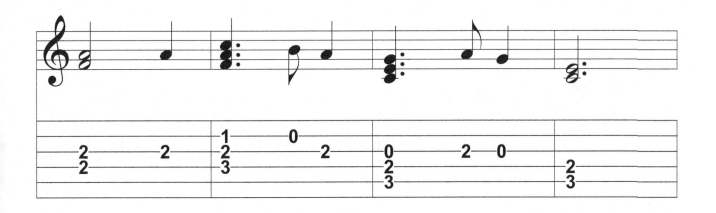
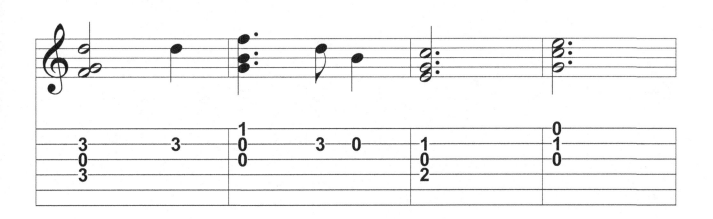
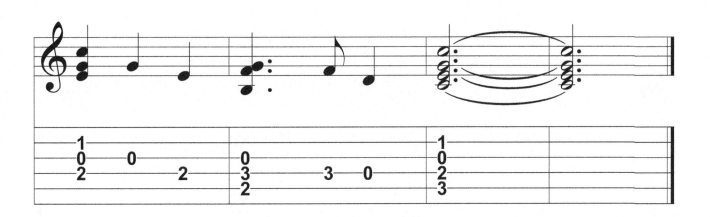

Silent Night

Silent Night

Up On the Housetop

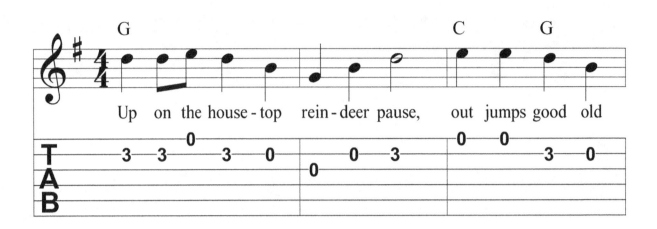
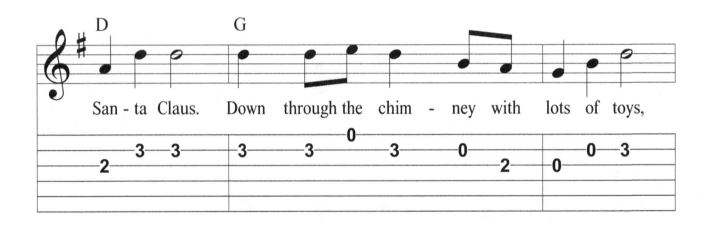
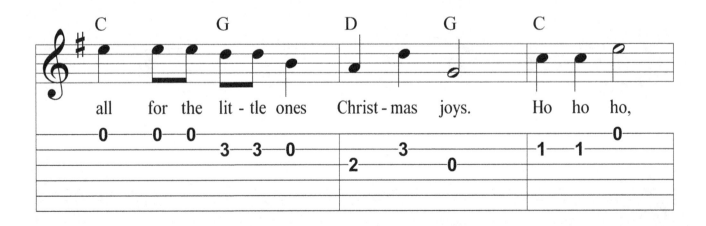

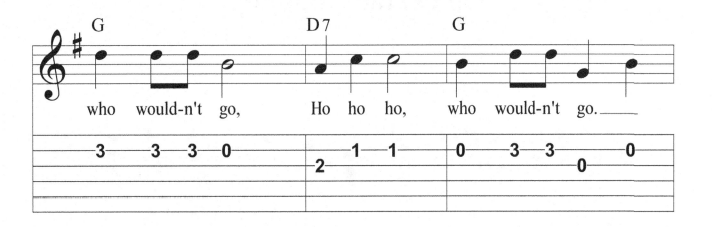
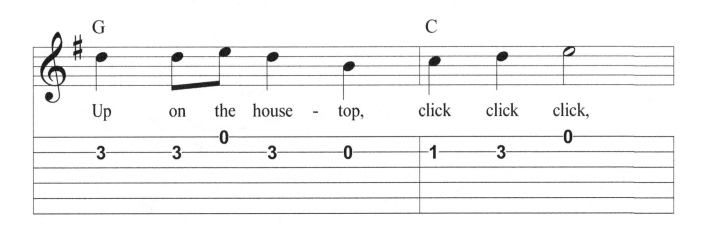
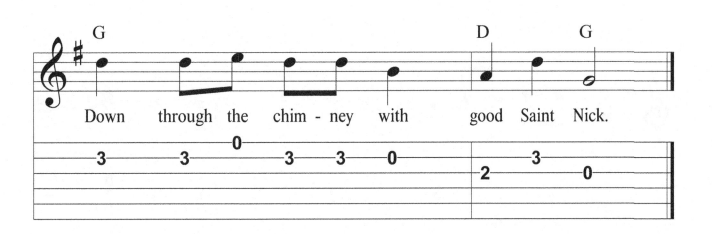

Up On the Housetop

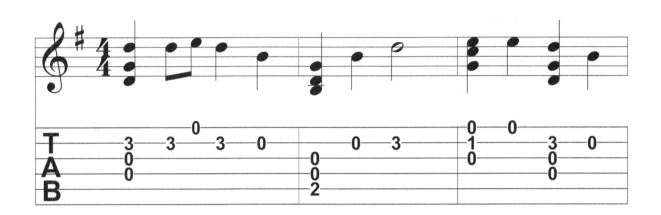

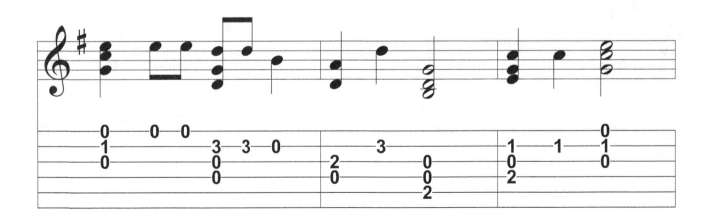

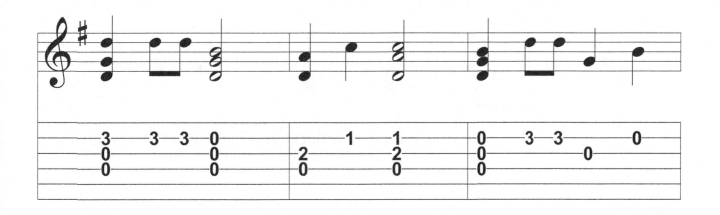

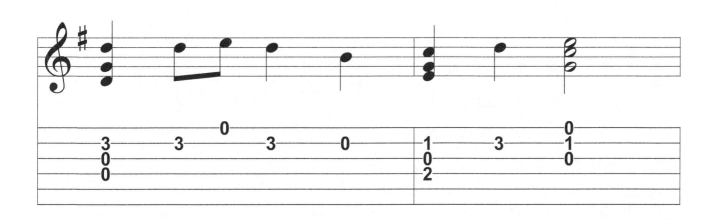

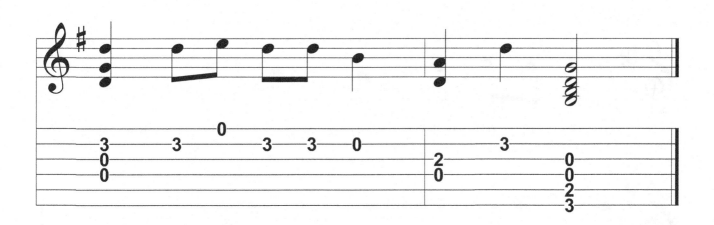

Up On the Housetop

Up On the Housetop

We Three Kings

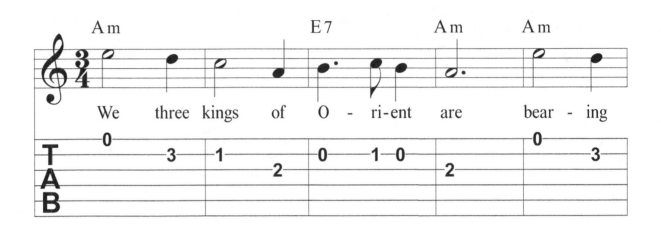
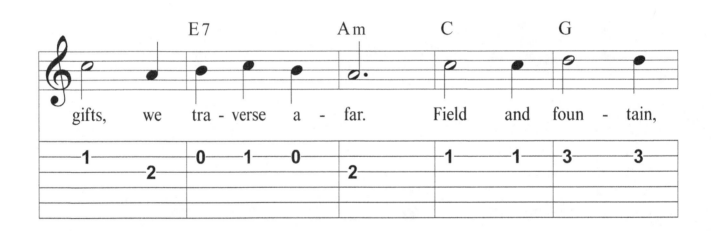
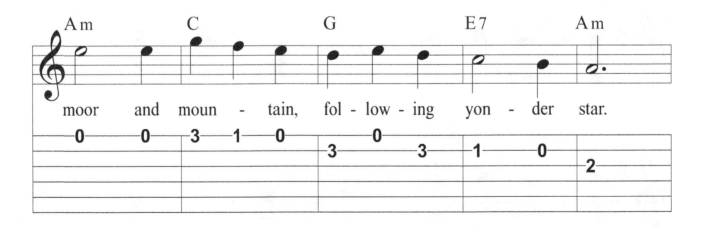

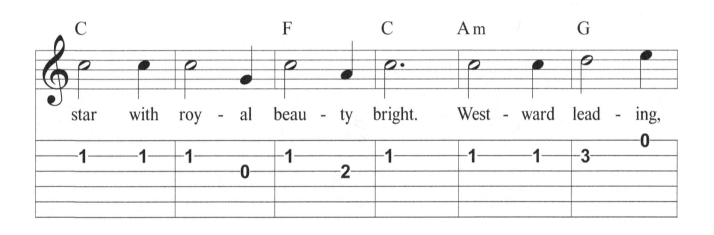
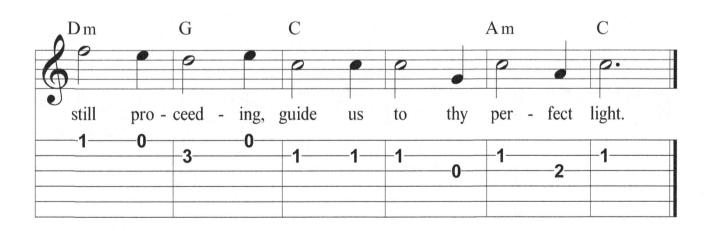

We Three Kings

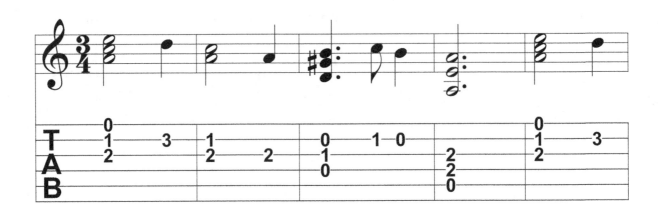
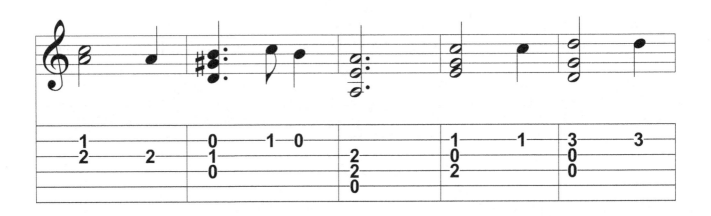
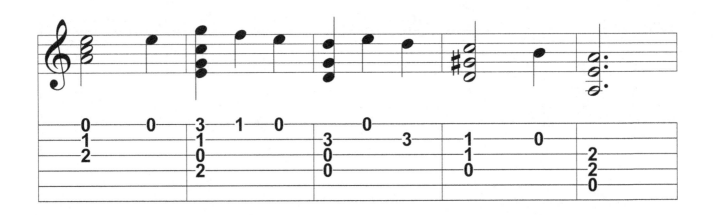

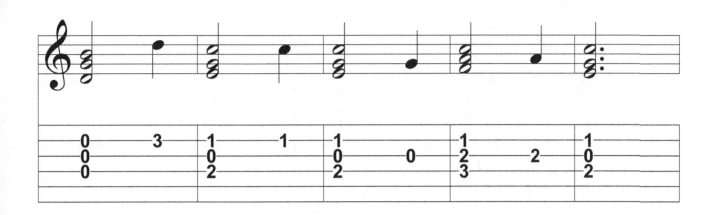

We Three Kings

We Three Kings

We Wish You a Merry Christmas

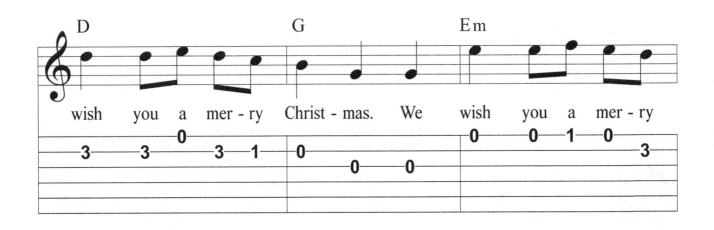
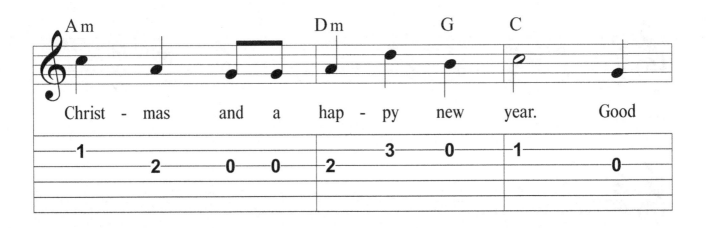

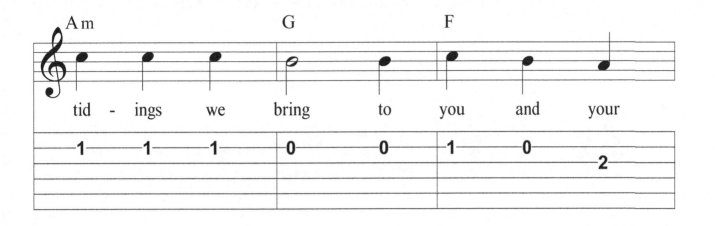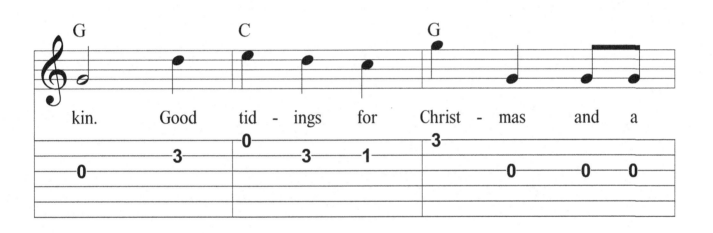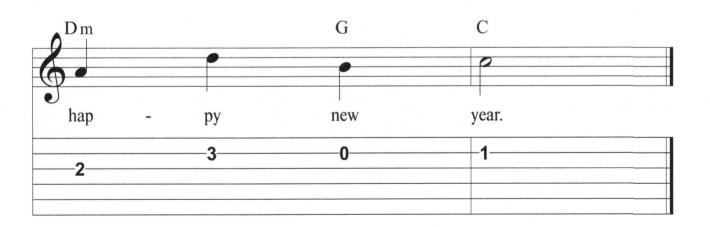

We Wish You a Merry Christmas

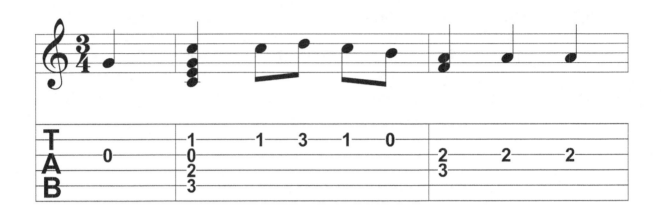
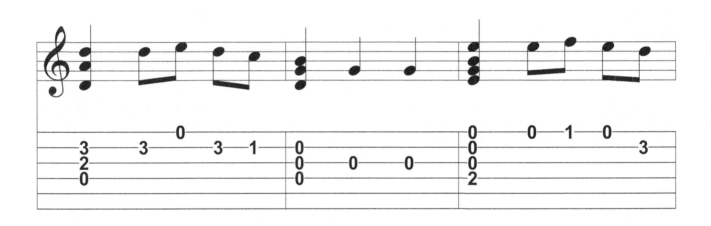
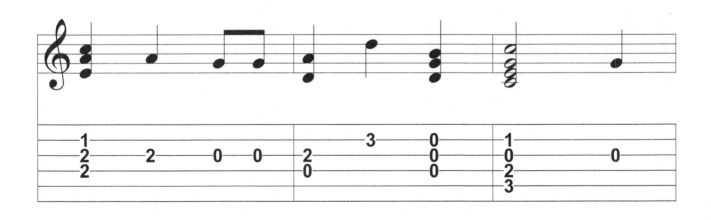

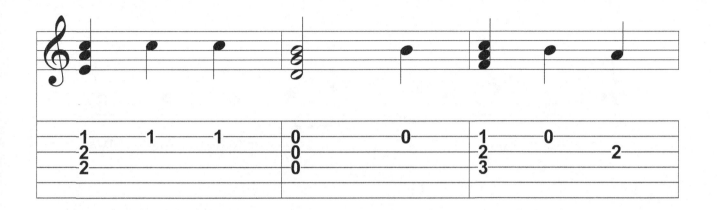
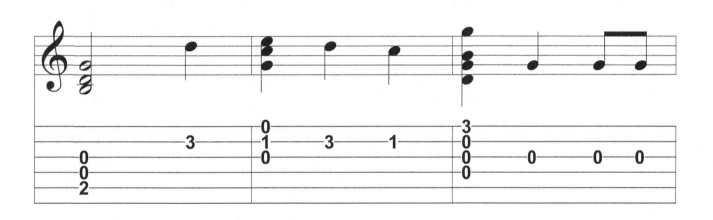
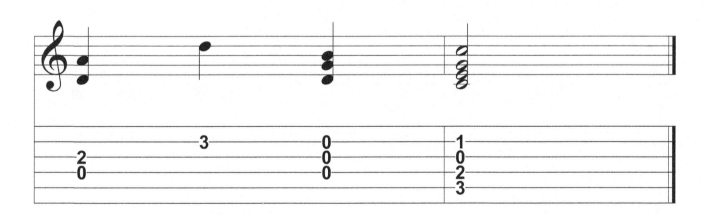

We Wish You a Merry Christmas

We Wish You a Merry Christmas

What Child is This?

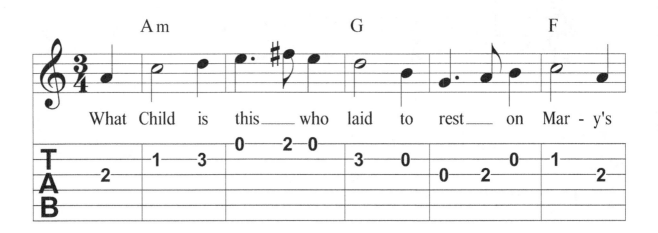
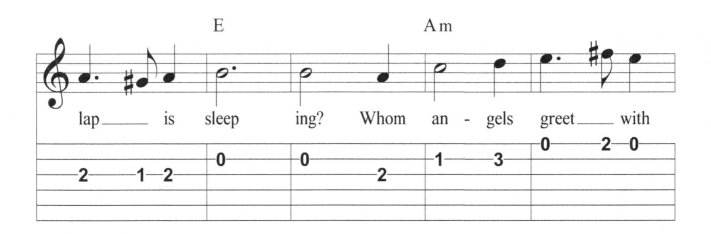
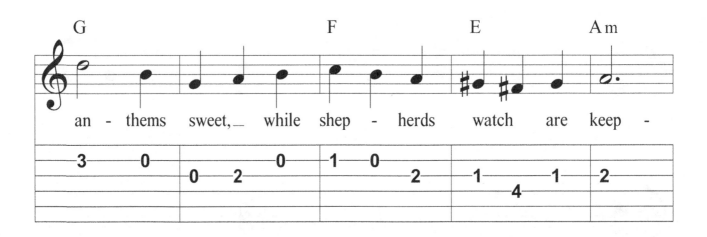

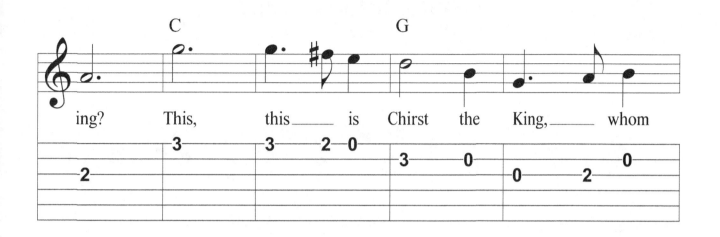
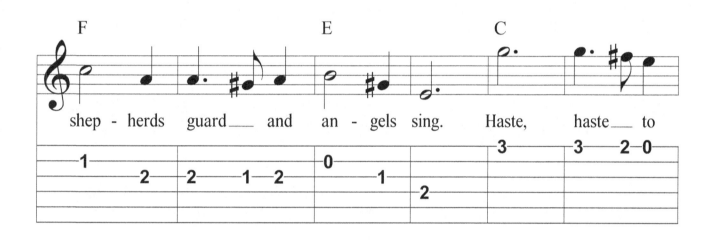
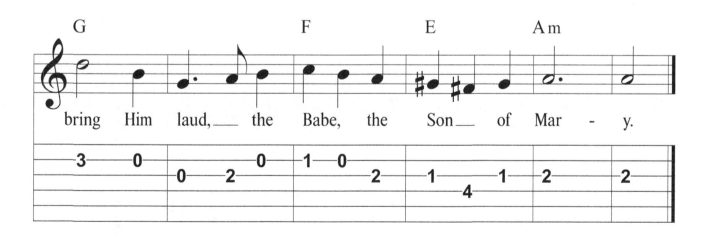

131

What Child is This?

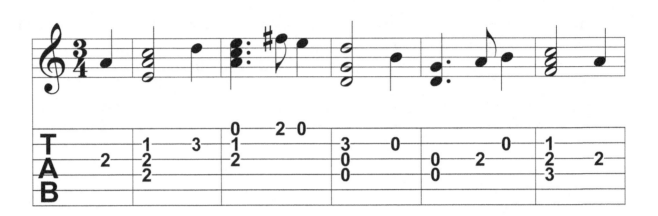
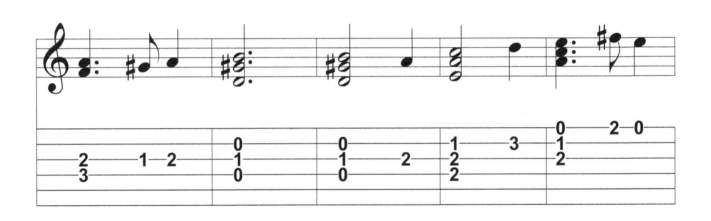

What Child is This?

134

What Child is This?

While Shepherds Watched Their Flocks

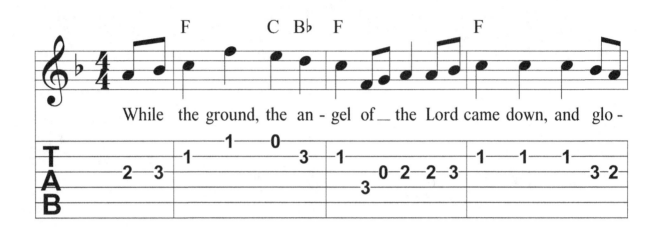
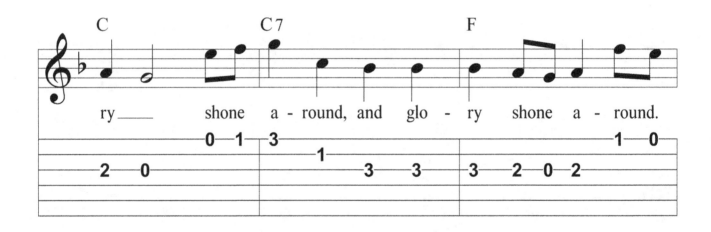
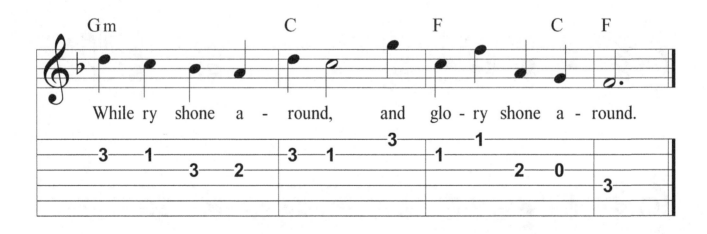

While Shepherds Watched Their Flocks

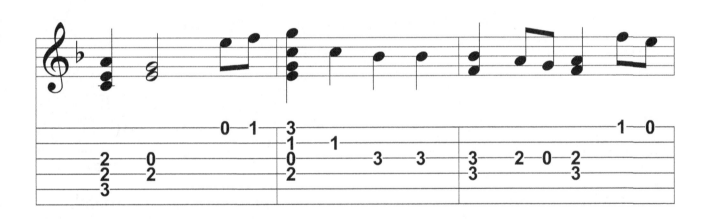

While Shepherds Watched Their Flocks

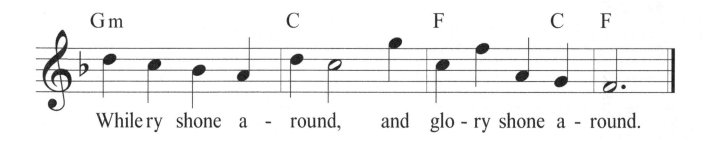

While Shepherds Watched Their Flocks

Also Available:

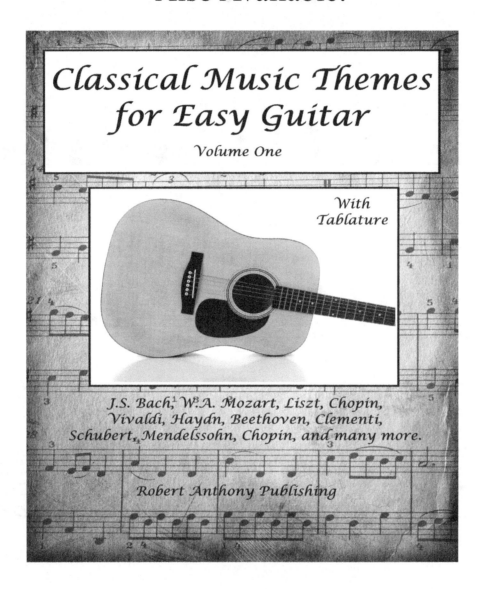

Featuring the music of:

J.S. Bach, Ludwig van Beethoven, Frédéric Chopin,
Claude Debussy, Franz Joseph Haydn, Franz Liszt,
Felix Mendelssohn, Leopold Mozart,
W.A. Mozart, Franz Schubert, Robert Schumann,
Pyotr Ilyich Tchaikovsky,
Richard Wagner, and more.

www.RobertAnthonyPublishing.com

Made in the USA
Las Vegas, NV
14 December 2023